MAHLER

Theodor W. Adorno

MAHLER

A Musical Physiognomy

Translated by Edmund Jephcott

THE UNIVERSITY OF CHICAGO PRESS   Chicago and London

The University of Chicago Press, Chicago 60637
The University of Chicago Press, Ltd., London
©1992 by the University of Chicago
All rights reserved. Published 1992
Paperback edition 1996
Printed in the United States of America

08 07 06 05 04 03 02 01 00 99   3 4 5 6 7 8 9 10

ISBN 0-226-00768-5 (cloth)
ISBN 0-226-00769-3 (paperback)

First published in Germany as *Mahler: Eine musikalische Physiognomik.*
©Suhrkamp Verlag, Frankurt am Main, 1971.

Library of Congress Cataloging-in-Publication Data

Adorno, Theodor W., 1903–1969.
   [Mahler, English]
   Mahler: a musical physiognomy / Theodor W. Adorno; translated by
Edmund Jephcott.
   p.   cm.
   Translation of: Mahler.
   Bibliography: p.
   1. Mahler, Gustav, 1860–1911—Criticism and interpretation.
I. Title.
ML410.M23A5513   1991
780′.92′4—dc19   88-14248
                                                                          CIP
                                                                          MN

CONTENTS

PREFACE
TO THE SECOND GERMAN EDITION

The text of the second edition is unchanged from the first, except for the correction of misprints.

It may be noticed that "Quasi una fantasia," the second volume of the author's musical writings, also contains two texts on Mahler.

One is a memorial address given at the invitation of the Gustav Mahler-Gesellschaft in June 1960 in Vienna. It was formulated after the completion of the book. This may have given it a certain quality of overview, of detachment from its subject, that justifies its retention alongside the book, which itself aspires to be as close as possible to its subject in the constellation of its individual analyses. It is the book alone that expresses the insight at which the author was aiming.

The "Epilegomena" should be read as additional and complementary material to the book. Many are concerned with the central complex of the Sixth Symphony. The reader may be reminded again that between this work and "Rewelge" the most profound connections exist, going far beyond scattered thematic echoes.

The fragment of the Tenth is deliberately not discussed in the book. The philological questions it poses are far too unresolved for the author to permit himself a judgment; without a decision on textual problems and an assessment of attempted reconstructions the subject itself could not be validly discussed. All that seems certain to the author is that even if the whole formal progression of the movements were established and all the sketches saved, they remain *vertically* fragmentary. Even in the opening Adagio, which is clearly the furthest advanced, sometimes only the harmonic "chorale" and one or two main parts are written down, the contrapuntal fabric being merely indicated. However, the layout of the work and the whole approach of Mahler's late style leave no doubt that it is only the harmonic polyphony, the tissue of voices within the framework of the chorale, that would have brought into being the concrete form of the music itself. If one strictly respects what originates from Mahler, one arrives at something incomplete and contradictory to his intention; but if one completes it contrapuntally, the adaptation usurps the true theater of Mahler's own productivity. Accordingly, the author inclines to the view that precisely someone who senses the extraordinary scope of the conception of the Tenth ought to do without adaptations and performances. The case is similar with sketches of unfinished pictures by masters: anyone who understands them and can visualize how they might have been completed would prefer to file them away and contemplate them privately, rather than hang them on the wall.

That the second edition was needed so quickly indicates that a full awareness of Mahler's importance is beginning to come about.

October 1963

MAHLER

1

The difficulty of revising the judgment on Gustav Mahler passed not only by the Hitler regime but by the history of music in the fifty years since the composer's death exceeds that which music generally presents to thought, and even to philosophical thought. Inadequate as is thematic analysis to the content of Mahler's symphonies —an analysis which misses the music's substance in its preoccupation with procedure—no more sufficient would be the attempt to pin down, in the jargon of authenticity, the statement put forward by the music. To try to grasp such a statement directly as something represented by the music would be to assign Mahler to the sphere of overt or tacit program music, which he early resisted and which has subsequently become plainly invalid. Ideas that are treated, depicted, or deliberately advanced by a work of art are not its ideas but materials—even the "poetic ideas" whose hazy designations were intended to divest the program of its coarse materiality. The fatuous sublimity of "What death told me," a title foisted on Mahler's Ninth, is even more distasteful in its distortion of a moment of truth than the flowers and beasts of the Third, which may well have been in the composer's mind. Mahler is particularly resistant to theorizing because he entirely fails to acknowledge the choice between technique and imaginative content. In his work a purely musical residue stubbornly persists that can be interpreted in terms neither of processes nor of moods. It informs the gestures of his music. To understand him would be to endow with speech the music's structural elements while technically locating the glowing expressive intentions. Mahler can only be seen in perspective by moving still closer to him, by entering into the music and confronting the incommensurable presence that defies the stylistic categories of program and absolute music no less than the bald historical derivation from Bruckner. His symphonies assist such closeness by the compelling spirituality of their sensuous musical configurations. Instead of illustrating ideas, they are destined concretely to become the idea. As each of their moments, tolerating no evasion into the approximate, fulfills its musical function, it becomes more than its mere existence: a script prescribing its own interpretation. The curves so enjoined are to be traced by contemplation, rather than by ratiocination on the music from an ostensibly fixed standpoint external to it, in the pharisaic manner of the "New Objectivity," tirelessly toying with clichés such as that of the titanic late Romantic.

The First Symphony opens with a long pedal point in the strings, all playing harmonics except for the lowest of the three groups of double basses. Reaching to the highest A of the violins, it is an unpleasant whistling sound like that emitted by old-fashioned steam engines. A thin curtain, threadbare but densely woven, it hangs from the sky like a pale gray cloud layer, similarly painful to sensitive eyes. In the third measure the motive of a fourth detaches itself, tinged by the piccolo. The ascetic asperity of the pianissimo is as precisely calculated as similar timbres to be heard seventy years later in Stravinsky's last scores, when the master of instrumentation tired of masterful instrumentation. After a second woodwind entry, the motive of the fourth descends sequentially until it comes to rest on a B-flat that clashes with the A of the strings. The tempo suddenly quickens with a pianissimo fanfare for two clarinets in their pale, lower register, with the weak bass clarinet as the third voice, sounding faintly as if from behind the curtain that it vainly seeks to penetrate, its strength failing. Even when the fanfare is taken up by the trumpets it still remains, as the score directs, *in sehr weiter Entfernung* (in the far distance)."[1] Then, at the height of the movement, six measures before the return of the tonic D, the fanfare explodes in the trumpets, horns, and high woodwinds,[2] quite out of scale with the orchestra's previous sound or even the preceding crescendo. It is not so much that this crescendo has reached a climax as that the music has expanded with a physical jolt. The rupture originates from beyond the music's intrinsic movement, intervening from outside. For a few moments the symphony imagines that something has become reality that for a lifetime the gaze from the earth has fearfully yearned for in the sky. With it Mahler's music has kept faith; the transformation of that experience is its history. If all music, with its first note, promises that which is different, the rending of the veil, his symphonies attempt to withhold it no longer, to place it literally before our eyes; they seek to rejoin musically and surpass the theatrical fanfare in the dungeon scene in *Fidelio*, to go beyond that A which, four measures before the trio, marks the caesura in the Scherzo of Beethoven's Seventh. So an adolescent woken at five in the morning by the perception of a sound that descends overpoweringly upon him may never cease to await the return of what was heard for a second between sleeping and waking. Its physical presence makes metaphysical thought appear as pale and feeble as an aesthetic that asks whether, in a formal sense, the moment of rupture has been successfully achieved or merely intended—a moment that rebels against the illusion of the successful work.

This causes Mahler to be hated today. It masquerades as an honest aversion to ostentation: to the art-work's claim to embody something merely added in thought, without being realized. Behind such scruples lies rancor against the very thing to be realized. The lament "It shall not be," over which Mahler's music despairs, is maliciously sanctioned as a precept. The insistence that there should be nothing in music other than what is present here and now cloaks both an embittered resignation and the complaisance of a listener who spares himself the exertion of comprehending the musical concept as something evolving, pointing beyond itself. Even at the time of "Les Six," an astute intellectual anti-Romanticism had formed a disreputable alliance with the entertainment sphere. Mahler enrages those who have made their peace with the world by reminding them of what they must exorcise. Animated by dissatisfaction with the world, his art omits to satisfy its norms, and in this the world rejoices. The breakthrough (*Durchbruch*) in the First Symphony af-

fects the entire form. The recapitulation to which it leads cannot restore the balance demanded by sonata form. It shrinks to a hasty
epilogue. The young composer's sense of form treats it as a coda,
without thematic development of its own; the memory of the main
idea drives the music swiftly to its end. But the abbreviation of the
recapitulation is prepared by the exposition, which dispenses with
multiplicity of forms and the traditional thematic dualism and so
needs no complex restitution. The idea of breakthrough, which dic-
tates the entire structure of the movement, transcends the traditional form while fleetingly sketching its outline.

But Mahler's primary experience, inimical to art, needs art in
order to manifest itself, and indeed must heighten art from its own
inner necessity. For the image corresponding to breakthrough is
damaged because the breakthrough has failed, like the Messiah, to
come into the world. To realize it musically would be at the same
time to attest to its failure in reality. It is in music's nature to over-
reach itself. Utopia finds refuge in its no man's land. What the immanence of society blocks cannot be achieved by an immanence of
form derived from it. The breakthrough sought to penetrate both. In
the entrapment that music would breach, it is itself entangled as art,
augmenting it through involvement in appearances. Music as art
transgresses against its truth; but it offends no less if, violating
art, it negates its own idea. Mahler's symphonies progressively seek
to elude this fate. Yet they are rooted in what music seeks to transcend, the opposite of music which is also its concomitant. The Fourth
Symphony calls it *weltlich' Getümmel* (worldly tumult),[3] Hegel the
perverse "course of the world" (*Weltlauf*)[4] which confronts consciousness in advance as something "hostile and empty." Mahler is
a late link in the tradition of European Weltschmerz. The aimlessly
circling, irresistible movements, the perpetual motion of his music,
are always images of the world's course. Empty activity devoid of
autonomy is the never-changing. In this musically still rather tepid
hell, a taboo is placed on novelty; it is a hell of absolute space. The
Scherzo of the Second Symphony conveyed this feeling, and to a
much greater degree that of the Sixth. Hope in Mahler always resides in change. Formerly the activity of the vigorous subject, re-

flecting socially useful work, inspired the classical symphony, though even in Haydn, and far more in Beethoven, it was rendered ambiguous by humor. Activity is not, as ideology teaches, merely the purposive life of autonomous people, but also the vain commotion of their unfreedom. In the late bourgeois phase this becomes the specter of blind functioning. The subject is yoked into the world's course without finding himself reflected in it or being able to change it; the hope that for Beethoven still throbbed in active life and allowed the Hegel of the *Phenomenology* finally to give the world's course precedence before the individual who only attained reality in it has deserted a subject thrown back powerlessly on his own resources. Against this background, Mahler's symphonies plead anew against the world's course. They imitate it in order to accuse; the moments when they breach it are also moments of protest. Nowhere do they patch over the rift between subject and object; they would rather be shattered themselves than counterfeit an achieved reconciliation. To begin with, Mahler conveys the externality of the world's course in terms of program music. The prototypical Scherzo of the Second Symphony, based on the *Wunderhorn* song of St. Anthony's sermon to the fishes, culminates in the instrumental outcry of one in despair.[5] The musical self, the "we" that sounds from the symphony, breaks down. Breath is drawn between this movement and the following one with the yearning human voice. All the same, Mahler was not content even then with the overconfident poetic contrast between transcendence and worldliness. In the course of its restless movement, with harsh wind choruses, the music makes itself vulgar.[6] Yet simply through the internal logic of the composition, Hegelian justice so far guides the composer's pen that the world's course takes on something of the self-propagating, enduring, death-resisting force of life itself, as a corrective to the endlessly protesting subject; as soon as the theme passes to the first violins, sound and melodic character extinguish all traces of vulgarity.[7] A passage in Natalie Bauer-Lechner's *Recollections of Gustav Mahler*, which is so pertinent in its details and reveals such insight into the problems of composition from the composer's standpoint that its authenticity ought to be accepted, allows us to surmise that Mahler was aware of the ambivalence of the relation between the subject and the world's course. With regard to an anecdote about Frederick the Great, he observed:

> It's all well and good that the peasant's rights are protected in spite of the King, but there's another side to the story. Let the miller and his mill be protected on their own ground—if only the millwheels didn't clatter so, thereby overstepping their boundaries most shamelessly and creating immeasurable havoc in the territory of someone else's mind![8]

The justice done to the subject can become objective injustice, and subjectivity itself, in empirical terms the nervous composer's sensitivity to noise, instructs him that the world's course—in the terms of the anecdote, absolute power—as against the abstract protection of personal rights, is not simply reprehensible, that, as Hegel perceived, it is not so bad as virtue imagines it. Aware at the musical level of the crude abstractness of the antithesis between the world's course and the breakthrough, Mahler gradually concretizes it, and so mediates it, through the internal structure of his compositions.

The Scherzo of the Third Symphony, like that of the Second, is prompted by animal symbolism. Its thematic core is taken from the early song "Ablösung im Sommer"; its music has the same quality of confused bustle as the fish sermon. This, however, is not answered by despair but by sympathy. The music comports itself like animals: as if its empathy with their closed world were meant to mitigate something of the curse of closedness. It confers utterance on the speechless by imitating their ways in sound, takes fright itself then ventures forward again with harelike caution,[9] as a fearful child identifies with the tiniest goat in the clock case that escapes the big bad wolf. When the postilion's horn is heard, the hush of the seething hubbub is composed as its background. It has a human timbre against the attenuated muted strings, the residue of creaturely bondage to which the alien voice would do no harm. When two French horns melodiously annotate the phrase,[10] the precarious artistic moment reconciles the irreconcilable. But the menacing rhythm of the tramping animals, oxen with linked hoofs dancing triumphal rounds, prophetically mocks the thin fragility of culture, as long as it nurtures catastrophes that could swiftly invite the forest to devour the devastated cities. At the end the animal piece puffs itself up once more in literary style by a kind of panic epiphany[11] of the basic motive in augmentation. Overall, it oscillates between pan-humanism and parody. Its light-beam falls on that perverted human condition that, under the spell of the self-preservation of the species, erodes its essential self and makes ready to annihilate the species by fatefully substituting the means for the end it has conjured away. Through animals humanity becomes aware of itself as impeded nature and of its activity as deluded natural history; for this reason Mahler meditates on them. For him, as in Kafka's fables, the animal realm is the human world as it would appear from the standpoint of redemption, which natural history itself precludes. The fairy-tale tone in Mahler is awakened by the resemblance of animal and man. Desolate and comforting at once, nature grown aware of itself casts off the superstition of the absolute difference between them. However, until Mahler art-music went in the opposite direction. The better it learned to master nature through the necessary mastery of its material, the more masterful its gestures became. Its integral oneness abolished multiplicity; its suggestive power severed all distractions. It preserved the image of happiness only by proscribing it. In Mahler it begins to rebel, seeks to make peace with nature, and yet must forever enforce the old interdiction.

The Scherzo of the Fourth Symphony, in line with the two preceding it, stylizes the sturdy allegory of worldly bustle into a dance of death. The shrill fiddle, tuned a tone higher than the violins, opens sinisterly with a bizarrely unfamiliar sound that irritates doubly, since the ear cannot account for its strangeness. Chromatic inflections sour the harmony and melody; the color is soloistic, as if something were missing: as if chamber music had parasitically invaded the orchestra. From images of baseness the music advances into unreality, phantasmagoric bustle ambiguously suspended between enticement and tears, mingling the sob of grief with its fleeting train of images. Similarly ambivalent is a melody of the woodwinds and later of the strings, a kind of *cantus firmus* to the hurrying main theme[12] of the Scherzo of the Seventh Symphony, which no longer has any pretense of innocence. Marked *klagend* (lamenting) by Mahler, it combines, as only music can, the barrel-organ grinding of the world's course with that which expressively mourns it. Mahler's sense of form compels him to place the break-through, traces of which have not been absent, in the Scherzo of the Fourth, as a contrast to its ghostliness, as an influx of reality, of blood, that has already been sought in passages of the trio that spontaneously assume the *Ländler* quality of the first theme. For a few seconds, *sich noch mehr ausbreitend*[13] (broadening still further), there is a sensuousness seldom found in Mahler; Tchaikovsky is skirted, then immediately left behind as the movement recoils further and further into the realm of the spectral and somber, with a conclusion from the imaginative horizon of the late Beethoven. Yet the serenity of the Fourth as a whole is always preserved. It mutes the macabre tone with an almost genial temperance.

Pressing to its conclusion the logic of the antithesis between the world's course and the breakthrough, at the height of the Fifth Symphony, in the second movement, Mahler raises it to a principle of composition. Paul Bekker recognized this as a kind of second first movement and as one of Mahler's most magnificent conceptions.[14] It is not a scherzo but a full sonata movement, of *größte Vehemenz*[15] (utmost vehemence). The humor that presumed, from a distance accorded to no one, to smile at the world's course has been swept away; the movement is driven along irresistibly, with all the accents of suffering unappeased. Its proportions, the relation of the tempestuous allegro passages to the proliferating slow intrusions from the Funeral March, make it uncommonly difficult to perform. These proportions cannot be left to chance simply as what the composer ordained; from the outset the whole piece must be so clearly organized around the contrast that it does not lose momentum in the andante sections; the changes constitute its form. It is of especial importance that even the presto passages should be played distinctly, their whirling themes intact, without compromising the tempo; they balance the melodies of the Funeral March. Yet it is the formal principle of the headlong presto that it should lead nowhere. For all its dynamism and vivid detail, the movement has no history, no direction, and really no emphatic dimension of time. Its lack of historical progress inclines it toward reminiscence; its energy, blocked in its forward rush, seems to flow backwards. Yet from there the music comes to meet it. The dynamic potential of the Funeral March, particularly of its second trio, is unfolded only retrospectively in a coherent, sonata-like through-composition, as a pendant to the presto. What was fettered in the static form of the first movement is now released. But at the same time the interrupting reminiscences prepare for the chorale vision that saves the movement from circularity. Only through the formal correspondence between this vision and the low interpolations can the movement assimilate the irrupting element without reverting to chaos. Vision and form determine each other. The latter closes with a coda. The vision has no conclusive force. Had it ended the movement, it would no longer have been a vision. But the coda reflects all that has gone before; in it the old storm finds a harmless echo.

The fanfare of the breakthrough takes on musical form as a chorale, no longer as alien territory but thematically mediated to the whole. However, the effect owes its power not only to the composition itself but to an allusion to the close of Bruckner's Fifth Symphony and so to the established authority of the symphonic use of the chorale. This reveals the impossibility of the possible even in the midst of mastery. The apparition is marred by appearances. What ought to be entirely itself bears the mark of consolation and exhortation: reassurance from something not present. Impotence attends manifested power; were it the promised and no longer the promise, it would not need to assert itself as power. For Mahler's music, nothing was so unquestioned in the traditional canon of forms as to allow his paradoxical intention to take refuge in them. The words of the last scene of *Faust*, which Mahler later set incomparably to music, are here violated. The end has not been achieved. The utopian identity of art and reality has foundered. But it is to this failure that Mahler's music henceforth addresses itself, no less earnestly in its technical progress than in its disenchanting experience. The artistic obligation that occasioned his aversion to the redundancies of the program constrains him to elaborate the breakthrough in strictly musical terms, to shed his naïve hostility to art, until the breakthrough itself becomes an intrinsic element of form. However, his concept is not inviolable. It is in the logic of composition to criticize what it seeks to represent; the more achieved the work, the poorer grows hope, for hope seeks to transcend the finitude of the harmoniously self-sufficient work. Something of this dialectic is present in all that is called maturity, unqualified praise of which is always corruptible by resignation. This is the affliction of aesthetic judgment. Through the insufficiency of the successful work the insufficient one, condemned by that judgment, becomes significant. It is doubtful, in view of the rift between the world's course and that which is other, whether there is more truth where that Other is manifested without pretense that the subject attains realization through the work, escaping illusion by confessing to its illusoriness—or where the internal coherence of the work simulates a coherence of meaning, insisting on its own truth, only to become in its entirety a deception, nourished by all the illusion of detail that it had eradicated. Nevertheless, music should not be impervious to its own logic. It is not by accident that the D major chorale in the second movement of the Fifth once more has the phantasmagoric quality of a celestial apparition. The residue of musically redundant material in it mars the supra-aesthetic sphere represented by the chorale: it incurs the taint of entertainment. To increase its power, the chorale is entrusted to the brass, debased since Wagner and Bruckner by empty bombast. Mahler was the last to overlook this. Musical integration, the elimination of all surplus intention, for him involves the criticism of appearances, which became explicit in Schoenberg and his school. Nothing, perhaps, more exactly characterizes the advancing sublimation of Mahler's sensibility than his increasingly strict abstention from underscoring main themes in the New German manner with brass. The experienced conductor may have been influenced in this by the technical consideration that such devices, like all well-proven effects, soon wear out, even in his own symphonies. All themes trumpeted by the brass bear a fatal resemblance to each other, endangering what is most important in a symphony, the individuality of details and thus the clear delineation of the musical process. In the late works violent effects in the brass become something isolated, disturbing, or overwhelming; they are no longer a basic element in the total sound. However, the sublimation of the breakthrough, although necessitated technically, is also founded teleologically within the breakthrough itself. If it is to be authentically enacted, the whole piece must be orientated toward it. Not only is the musical fiber molded around it, but each moment necessarily has a functional relation to it, being thus divested more and more of its literal, crudely material meaning. In the First Symphony, which reveals but does not resolve the tensions within Mahler's music, this is seen clearly. The recapitulation after the breakthrough cannot be the simple recapitulation formally required. The return that the breakthrough evokes must be its result: something new. To prepare for this musically, a new theme is evolved in the development, the melodic germ of which is introduced at the start in the cellos.[16] From it an episodic horn phrase is formed[17] and then, like a "model" in Beethoven, it dominates the later development to emerge retrospectively, as it were, at the return of the tonic, as the main theme which, at the time, it never was.[18] It no less meets the obligation, enjoined by the fanfare, to be something new than it provides the secret source throughout the music's protracted evolution, at once in the spirit of the sonata and against it, of the entire piece. For the sake of the breakthrough, of the Other, formal integration is increased, blunting the absolute antithesis that the breakthrough demands.

Viennese classicism was incapable of this antithesis, as was any musical attitude to which the concept of philosophical idealism could be applied. For Beethoven's mighty logic, music composed itself as a seamless identity, an analytical judgment. The philosophy informing such music began, at its Hegelian apogee, to feel the spur of the new idea. In a note on the theory of Ground in the *Science of Logic,* the grounds of scientific thought—Kant is not mentioned—are criticized for not moving "off the spot," amounting to tautologies: because

> this procedure fits [the ground] to the phenomenon and its derivatives rest upon the latter, so that this naturally flows from its ground smoothly and with a fair wind. But knowledge has not been advanced; it drifts in a distinction of form which this very procedure reverses and cancels.[19]

Common sense, abstracting its explanations from facts that exist in any case, is denounced as stupid. Against it Mahler rebels. If music indeed has more in common with dialectical than with discursive logic, it seeks in him to attain what philosophy strives with Sisyphean labors to wrest from traditional thought, from concepts hardened to a rigid identity. His Utopia is the forward motion of the past and the not-yet-past in becoming. As it was for Hegel in his critique of the principle of identity,[20] truth for Mahler is the Other, which is not immanent yet arises from immanence; in a similar way Kant's doctrine of synthesis was reflected in Hegel. To be is to have become, as against merely becoming. The economic principle of traditional music, however, its kind of determination, exhausts itself in exchanging one thing for another, leaving nothing behind. It "comes out" but has no outcome. Anything new that it cannot wholly assimilate it shuns. Seen in this way, even great music before Mahler was tautological. Its correctness was that of a system without contradictions. It is consigned to the past by Mahler, the breach becoming a formal law. "What is different you now shall learn."[21]

If Mahler's development as a composer mediates between the world's course and that which is other, the mediation, in order to go deep enough, should be detectable in the substance of his music itself. This substance is what the world's course acts upon, taking its movement from it, yet not quite resembling it; it is the subjugated that remains below ground or has been repressed. There Mahler's music hopes, with a Romanticism that affects the language of music itself and is thereby radicalized, for an immediateness that would soothe the pain of estrangement inherent in universal mediation. Originally, the fanfares used the natural tones of the brass. In the introduction to the First Symphony, where the clarinets anticipate the fanfare, they are immediately joined by natural sounds: the descending fourth that has always been considered natural, an unarticulated crescendo and diminuendo of the upward-straining oboes, cuckoo calls from the woodwinds, intruding regardless of rhythm and tempo, as they were to do again and again in Mahler. His symphonic writing seeks to catch the disordered voices of living things down to the farewell song ("Der Abschied") in *Das Lied von der Erde,* with its urge toward the amorphous. What is beyond form is akin through form to the still formless; the parousias of the supernatural, in which an excess of meaning is discharged, are composed of fragments of the natural bereft of meaning. But Mahler's vigilant music is unromantically aware that mediation is universal. Even the nature it woos is a function of what it shuns; without a mediating consciousness, fate and myth would have the last word. Since aesthetics has taken to neglecting natural beauty, to which Kant still reserved the category of the sublime while Hegel despised it, the concept of nature has gone unnoticed in art. The net of socialization has been woven so tightly since then that its mere antithesis is guarded as a sacred mystery that cannot be discussed. For nature, although the opposite of human domination, is itself distorted as long as it is exposed to want and violence. Even where Mahler's music arouses associations of nature and landscape, it nowhere presents them as absolutes, but infers them from the contrast to that from which they deviate. Technically, the natural sounds are relativized by their departure from the syntactical regularity otherwise prevalent in Mahler: his musical prose is not primarily such, but proliferates as a free rhythm on the verse. For him nature, as the definite negation of music's artistic language, is dependent on this language. The tormenting pedal point at the start of the First Symphony presupposes the official ideal of good instrumentation in order to reject it. In his search for estrangement Mahler only hit on the use of harmonics for that note after the event:

> When I heard the A in all registers in Budapest, it sounded far too substantial for the shimmering and glimmering of the air that I had in mind. It then occurred to me that I could have all the strings play harmonics (from the violins at the top, down to the basses, which also possess harmonics). Now I had the effect I wanted.[22]

Natalie Bauer-Lechner relates a very plausible statement indicating how far Mahler's technical method was guided consciously by such positive negation, by protest against the accepted ideal of musical beauty:

> If I want to produce a soft, subdued sound, I don't give it to an instrument which produces it easily, but rather to one which

> can get it only with effort and under pressure—often only by
> forcing itself and exceeding its natural range. I often make the
> basses and bassoon squeak on the highest notes, while my
> flute huffs and puffs down below. There's a passage like this in
> the fourth movement—you remember the entry of the vi-
> olas? . . . I always enjoy this effect; I could never have pro-
> duced that powerful, forced tone if I had given the passage to
> the cellos (the most obvious choice here).[23]

As in their relation to the comfortable normal sound, Mahler's nature passages can be defined in general as exacerbated deviations
from high musical language, just as natural beauty itself stands in
relation to the supposedly purified formal categories of taste: as a
denaturing of second nature. Likewise, the flaws in musical logic, at
which Mahler's self-criticism is directed, are produced by an intention that walks the narrow ridge of meaning between the absurd
and the qualitatively new. Mahler already plays desultorily with
chance. Elements of nature scattered in his art always have an un-
natural effect: only by the exaggeration it undergoes everywhere in
Mahler's compositions can the compositional tone repel the convention that the formal language of Western music had become in
Mahler's age, while still feeling at home in that convention. It robs
the music of innocence. Through the contrast between the disrup-
tive intention and the musical language, the latter is transformed
unobserved from an a priori convention into an expressive means:
in a similar way Kafka's pointedly conservative, objectively epic
prose schooled in Kleist accentuates its content by contrasting with it.

The emerging antagonism between music and its language reveals a rift within society. The irreconcilability of the inward and the
outward can no longer be harmonized spiritually, as in the classical
age. This induces in Mahler's music the unhappy consciousness that
that age believed overcome. The historical hour no longer allows it
to see human destiny as reconcilable in the existing conditions with
the institutional powers that force human beings, if they would earn
their livings, into conditions contrary to them in which they can nowhere find themselves. This message was hammered, to the point of
physical destruction, into a composer confined to the vacation

months by a music business that even as Director of the Vienna Opera and star conductor he did not cease to despise. Mocked by reality,
the sublime degenerates into ideology. This is why Mahler's relation to the vulgar becomes dialectical. To be sure, he wrote: "Music
must always contain a yearning, a yearning for what is beyond the
things of this world."[24] But his symphonies discern better than he
that the object of such yearning is not to be represented as something higher, noble, transfigured. It would otherwise become a Sunday religion, a decorative justification of the world's course. If the
Other is not to be sold off, it must be sought incognito, among lost
things. According to this conception, it is not what exalts itself
above the business of self-preservation, from which it profits, that
escapes the nexus of guilt, but what has gone under, bears the burden, and is thereby spurred to exert the counterpressure that the
coincidentia oppositorum of Mahler's music combines with the
Utopian explosive. Disgusted by his own position, he was still unwilling to renounce it, knowing the world's course too well not to be
always aware that want could deprive him of that margin of freedom
needed by his condition as a human being. The socialistic inclina-
tions of the successful composer belong to an era in which the pro-
letariat has already been incorporated. The instinct of the peddler's
grandson does not make common cause with those forming the bat-
talions of the stronger but, in however despairing and illusory a
manner, with the margins of society. The undomesticated element
in which Mahler's music collusively immerses itself is also archaic,
outdated. This is why a music inimical to compromise bound itself
to traditional material. It was thereby reminded of the victims of
progress, even musical victims: those elements of language ejected
by the process of rationalization and material control. It was not the
peace disturbed by the world's course that Mahler sought in that
language; rather, he endowed it with power in order to resist power.
The shabby residue left by triumph accuses the triumphant. Mahler
sketches a puzzle composed of the progress that has not yet begun,
and the regression that no longer mistakes itself for origin.

2

Mahler's progressiveness does not reside in tangible innovations and advanced material. Opposed to formalism, he prefers what is actually composed to the means of composition and so follows no straight historical path. Even in his own day all individual qualities, those best things he would not forget, threatened to be leveled into the bare unity of organization. The totality only appeals to him when it results from irreplaceable musical details. Just as his symphonies cast doubt on the inherent logic of musical identity, they also oppose that historical verdict that since *Tristan* has driven music on unidimensionally: chromatization as the removal from the material of all individual qualities. Not as a reactionary but as if shunning the price of progress, he insists on the diatonic as a sure foundation when it has already been shaken by the demands of autonomous composition. Despite the belated innocence of their material, however, his works, from their first appearance, were felt to give offense. The hatred of Mahler, with anti-Semitic overtones, was not so different from that of the New Music. The shock he administered was dissipated in laughter, a malign refusal to take his music seriously that repressed the knowledge that there was something in it after all. It is true of Mahler as of almost no other that what exceeds accepted standards also falls slightly short of them; the refined taste of musical academicians, headshakingly, is apt to convict Mahler's breakthroughs of childishness. Mahler did not bow unconditionally to the Wagnerian wish that music should finally come of age. Dreamlike infallibility and the infantile cannot be clearly distinguished in him. When Debussy walked out of the Paris première of the Second Symphony in protest, the sworn opponent of dilettantism behaved like a regular specialist; to him it may have sounded as Henri Rousseau's paintings looked among the Impressionists in the Jeu de Paume. Mahler cannot be reconciled with the notion of standard competence; while he at first is not in complete possession of it, he then violently shakes it in order to demolish its self-righteous prejudice, and finally cultural fetishism; not the least response is anger. All this was perpetrated within tonality. Perhaps alienation effects are only possible on somewhat familiar ground; if this is entirely relinquished, they too dissolve. The structure of Mahler's chords follows triadic harmony entirely; everywhere there are tonal centers of gravity, nowhere is the usual tonal idiom excluded. Much of this belongs to the years before the 1890's. In richness of texture (*Stufenreichtum*) the earlier symphonies at least are less demanding than Brahms, in chromaticism and enharmonic changes less than the mature Wagner. Mahler's atmosphere is the illusion of familiarity in which the Other is clothed. Timidly, with obsolete means, he anticipates what is to come.

What is new is his tone. He charges tonality with an expression that it is no longer constituted to bear. Overstretched, its voice cracks: a woodwind passage in the Scherzo of the Seventh Symphony, and an oboe part in "Rewelge" are marked *kreischend* (screeching) in the score. The forced tone itself becomes expressive. Tonality, the great category of musical mediation, had interposed itself as a conventional lubricant between the subjective intention and the aesthetic phenomenon. Mahler heats it up from within, from an expressive need, to the point that it again becomes incandescent, speaks, as if it were immediate. Exploding, it accomplishes what was later taken over by the emancipated dissonance of Expressionism. The first trio of the Funeral March of the Fifth Symphony, which already begins grandly enough, does not respond with a lyrical, subjective complaint to the objective lament of fanfare and march. It gesticulates, raises a shriek of horror at something worse than death. It is not surpassed by the frightful figures in Schoenberg's *Erwartung*. It draws its power, paradoxically, from the lack of a ready-made musical language for such experience. Through its troubled contrast to the innocent means it uses, that experience is more compelling than if the complaining dissonance were set completely free and so became the norm. In the mutually interrupting duet of the piercing trumpets and disordered violins, the gestures of the hetman, inciting to murder, are confused with the wails of the victims: pogrom music, much as the Expressionist poets prophesied the war. After the formally controlled march sections and the emphatic C-sharp minor, the expressive extremity of this passage, shunning the secure formal center, confers the same documentary status on the work that Schoenberg's *Survivor from Warsaw* was to achieve fifty years later. But at the same time tonality is seized upon reflectively as a means of expression. True, it had functioned in this way throughout the tonal era in every significant composer, especially in Beethoven, whenever subjective intentions needed to be objectified. But as Mahler makes the language of second nature eloquent, it is qualitatively transformed.

He disrupts the balance of tonal language. Among its elements he assiduously stresses and prefers one that is present among others but in no way outstanding, and only through its conspicuous use is filled with expression. From the early songs with piano to the Adagio theme in the Tenth Symphony, Mahler's persistent idiosyncrasies play with an alternation of the major and minor modes. It is the technical formula in which the excess of the poetic idea is encoded: from single phrases in which major and minor alternate abruptly, through the construction of motives, which, in the Sixth Symphony, selects the transition from major to minor, the lowering of the major to the minor third, as the unifying moment of the whole work, to the elaboration of large-scale forms, which—most strikingly in the first movement of the Ninth—are organized around the traditional dualism of major and minor sections. The melodic line, too, oscillates between major and minor thirds or other intervals possessing major–minor character, while preserving the same motives. This earned Mahler the charge of mannerism. Its rebuttal requires reflection on expression in music. This is not the expression of something specific; not by chance does the marking *espressivo* appear widely in his scores. It aims at marked intensity. It comes into the music from its remotest past, before the phase of rationality and unambiguous significance. As expression music behaves mimetically, as gestures respond to a stimulus that they imitate by reflex action. This mimetic moment in music gradually converges with the rational, the control of the material; how they have worn each other away is their history. They are not reconciled: in music too the rational, constructive principle suppresses the mimetic. The latter must assert itself polemically, posit itself; *espressivo* is the sanctioned, accepted protest of expression at the ban placed upon it. The more petrified the musical system of rationality, the less it accords expression its place. To be heard at all within tonality it must seize on an individual means, heighten it to an overvalued idea, harden it to a bearer of expression as the surrounding system is hardened. Mannerism is the scar left behind by expression in a language no longer capable of expression. Mahler's deviations are closely related to gestures of language; his peculiarities are clenched as in jargon. Some of the jerky repetitions of motives, at once violent and inhibited, in the major section of the Funeral March of the Fifth Symphony[1] are paradigmatic. Sometimes—and not merely in the recitative—Mahler's music has so completely mimed the gesture of speech that it sounds as if it were speaking literally, as was once promised, in musical Romanticism, by the title of Mendelssohn's *Songs without Words*. In the trio of the Scherzo in the Seventh Symphony, entirely a major–minor section, instrumental song phrases sing an imaginary text.[2] Extreme proximity to language is one of the roots of Mahler's symbiosis of song and symphony, in which nothing changed even in the instrumental middle symphonies. The Fifth, for example, quotes one of the *Kindertotenlieder*[3] in its first movement; the second trio of the Scherzo is of the type of major-mode sections in 'Wo die schönen Trompeten blasen"; the Adagietto, actually a song without words, is linked to "Ich bin der Welt abhanden gekommen," and one of the main motives in the Rondo Finale is taken from the *Wunderhorn* song against the critics ("Lob des Hohen Verstandes"). Song and symphony meet in the mimetic sphere that exists prior to neatly separated genres. The song's melody does not duplicate the words' meaning but assigns it to a collective tradition. And the instrumental and vocal elements in

Mahler are not of unmixed nature; the instruments cling to the singing voice, while the latter moves in a presubjective, melismatic way as it was only to do again in a late phase of the New Music. Guido Adler speaks of the "words accompanying his music,"[4] as against the "accompaniment of words by music," which rests on the reification of both. All categories are eroded in Mahler, none is established within unproblematic limits. Their dissolution does not arise from a lack of articulation but revises it: neither the distinct nor the blurred is defined conclusively; both are in suspension. As the overplayed expression cuts its traces in the material, it is in turn overtaken by traces of the reified, conventional, and sentimental. By demanding something genuine from a language that is, so to speak, precritical, still accepted but no longer able to support expression, he becomes incommensurable with Classicism. The complexion of his music repels a synthesis without contradictions. Its opposite, that which perennially resists fusion, is called manner; it testifies to an attempt that is ever renewed and ever in vain. The layer of reification in Mahler's music, implacably opposing the illusory reconciliation of antagonistic elements within the unreconciled, is not a mark of musical inadequacy but embodies a content that refuses to be dissolved in form. Mahler's major–minor manner has its function. It sabotages the established language of music with dialect. Mahler's tone has the flavor evoked by the Austrian dialect term *schmeckert* as applied to the Riesling grape. Its aroma, at once mordant and fugitive, assists spiritualization by its evanescence. This fluctuating, ambivalent tone in which, as in the popular *Freischütz*, love and grief are always apt to go hand in hand, technically presupposes a relation of major to minor that cannot be forced to a decision. The modality is left open, as if coming from a primeval world in which antithetical principles have not yet hardened to logical opposites. The disunity, the sorrow pervading even the joyful impulse, cannot, however, be reduced, as in the cheap interpretation of Mahler, to the composer as psychological subject, but is a form of reaction to the experience of the real, an attitude toward reality comparable to gallows humor—which, incidentally, was not unknown to Mahler. There is constant prattle about Mahler's music as a mirror of his soul. We read in the introduction to a recent

Kletzki recording of the Ninth Symphony, for example, that in it Mahler gave musical expression to his "inner personal problems" and that "when people talk about their souls the result is not always uniformly profitable."[5] Wisdom of this sort perorates on Mahler as a "tragic figure" and, while shedding crocodile tears of gratuitous condescension over his allegedly split self, betrays the rancor that always inhabits gestures of appreciation. Mahler's "inner personal problems" may not, to their advantage, have been "uniformly profitable" for his music, but they certainly damaged it less than the barbaric cut in the second movement of that otherwise far from worthless recording; the mention of them says more about the helplessness of intellectual historians in the face of intellectual formations than about the formations themselves. However self-evident the spirit pervading Mahler's and all more recent music may be, however little he is content to play with wallpaper patterns of animated sound, no more are his symphonies chained, in their urge toward divestment and totality, to a private person who, in reality, made himself an instrument in order to produce them. The repulsive counterpart to the image of the divided Mahler is that of the composing subject as a blond Siegfried, a balanced, harmonious individual who is supposed, singing like a bird, to shower as much happiness on his listeners as is falsely ascribed to him. The cliché comfortably matches the opposite one of Beethoven titanically grappling, for heaven knows what reason, with himself, and emerging victorious in the end. But the quality of music is not proved by the dubious achievement of the joy-bringer. It ranks higher the more deeply it is steeped in the contradictoriness of the world, which also marks the subject. It becomes more than merely contradictory when by aesthetic synthesis it transforms the tensions it harbors into the image of a truly attainable oneness. It is not as if Mahler the person, or even the immanent subject of his compositions, were free of conflicts. The traumatic tone in Mahler's music, a subjective moment of brokenness, is not to be denied, and secured him against the ideology of *mens sana in corpore sano*. But even where the musical process seems to say "I," its correlative, analogous to the latent objective first person of the literary narrative, is divided by the gulf of the aesthetic from the person who wrote the phrase. Mahler did not treat the wound as expressive content as Wagner did in the third act of *Tristan*. It is manifested objectively in the musical idiom and forms. In this way the shadow of negativity in his symphonies is made palpable. However, the wound of the person, what the language of psychology calls the neurotic character, was at the same time a historical wound, insofar as his work sought with aesthetic means to realize what was already aesthetically impossible. He did not legitimize himself in the slightest by deriving productivity from the defect itself, by raising the psychological fissures to objective ones. Residual whims of the subject are to be found in his music where it has not been entirely objectified, but it is not a seismogram of the soul. Music only became that in Expressionism. Instead, in Mahler, that subjective notion that feels music physically like a rushing in the head is met once more by the objective world, disembodied, impervious to concepts, yet utterly definite and clear. It is not so much that subjectivity is communicated or expressed by music as that in it, as in a theater, something objective is enacted, the identifiable face of which has been obliterated. It is rather that an orchestra plays within musical consciousness than that a consciousness is projected onto the orchestra. Perhaps this externality of the internal element of music endows it with the capacity, by which psychoanalysis would seek to explain it, to resist paranoia, to exorcise pathic narcissism. It is only another aspect of the same state of affairs that, to those who understand the language of music, obscures its meaning: mere meaning would be only an image of that subjectivity whose claims to omnipotence music abolishes. The dignity of Mahler's musical language lies in the fact that it can be entirely understood and understands itself, but eludes the hand that would grasp what has been understood. Not through its individual intentions, but only through the tissue in which they light up and fade, is this medium accessible to thought, in its totality. Mahler's music does not express subjectivity, but in it the latter takes up its stance toward objectivity. In his major–minor manner a relation to the world's course is distilled: aloofness from what violently rejects the subject, longing for it, after the final reconciliation of outward and inward. The rigid polar moments are mediated within the musical material, and their weft produces the tone. The long neutralized minor, sedimented as a formal element in the syntax of Western music, only becomes a symbol of mourning when modally awakened by the contrasting major. Its nature is that of divergence; in isolation it no longer produced this effect. As a deviation, the minor defines itself equally as the not integrated, the unassimilated, the not yet established. In the contrast between the two modes in Mahler, the divergence between the particular and the general is inextricably congealed. Minor is the particular, major the general; the Other, the deviant, is, with truth, equated with suffering. In the major–minor relationship, therefore, the expressive content is precipitated in sensuous, musical form. The price of this is a regression: what Mahler demands once more of the developed language of musical art is nothing other than what once gave birth to major and minor. This awakening to life is the figure of the new in Mahler's music. Tonality, permanently sharpened in the play of major and minor, becomes a medium of modernism. The ambivalence of the mode is already a criticism of tonality insofar as it forces it, through regression, to the point where it expresses what it can no longer express; in Schoenberg, too, tonality was breached not by being softened but constructively exerted. Mahler's minor chords, disavowing the major triads, are masks of coming dissonances. But the impotent weeping that contracts in them, and is rebuked as sentimental because it acknowledges impotence, dissolves the formula's rigidity, opens itself to the Other, whose unattainability induces weeping.

Mahler's means of representation is tonality as a whole, and primarily the major–minor dualism; this dualism is adopted for the sake of deviations, the ferment of a particular that is not absorbed in the general, and for that very reason needs the general as a framework of reference on which it can be plotted and from which it differs. What is general in Mahler's compositions in the end are the deviations themselves. The tone is not established—as in exemplary fashion in Brahms—by the articulation of all available means, but by intrusions, which irritate unquestioned tradition. Academic music theory speaks of "recognized" chords and the like. Mahler's music teems with them, with assimilated and yet not quite native elements, with harmonic and melodic incidents, chromatic scale degrees and passing notes, intrusions of the minor in major passages, intervals from the harmonic minor scale in the melodic line. He uses a battery of artistic devices long tolerated by diatonicism like foreign words but not one with it and which by their preponderance undermine it, as if the rational order of music were either not yet quite established or were already crumbling. On many occasions his predilection for such moments offends the norms of good musicianship. The earlier Mahler disregards the elementary academic demand for a powerful progression of degrees. He accumulates pedal points, basses that swing between tonic and dominant as in marches and popular dances, and he dislocates chords so that they move in parallel motion, especially in parallel fifths. For him, as somewhat later for Puccini and Debussy, the base line no longer has any real authority. He also shows a striking aversion to modulation, which never quite left him. Originally it may have been simple inexperience; but in significant artists what started as a defect is turned to account when it persists. That modulation played a relatively subordinate role for Mahler—with important exceptions, particularly in the Sixth, Seventh, and Ninth Symphonies—takes on musical significance. With regard to the vertical, too, Mahler seldom proceeds in an analytical, differentiating way. He does not organize his work through harmony in detail, but uses harmony to create light and shadow in the whole, effects of foreground and depth, perspective. For this reason tonal areas are more important to him than seamless transitions between them, or the fine harmonic articulation of each surface in itself: his harmony is macrological. Abrupt shifts are preferred to imperceptible modulations. The idea of macrological harmony affects even the structure of whole symphonies. In the Seventh the first movement, after an introduction reaching far ahead tonally, is in E minor. The three middle movements—all, including the Scherzo, night pieces—then descend to the subdominant region. The first *Nachtmusik* is at home in C major, the subdominant tonality of the relative major of E minor; the Scherzo falls further into D minor, the relative minor of the subdominant of C; the second *Nachtmusik*, finally, remains on the same harmonic level, but brightens it by replacing the D minor by its relative major, F. The Finale restores the balance between the first and the middle movements. These, however, exert a weight that the Finale cannot quite compensate. It must remain a dominant within the relative tonality of the first movement, and so be in the C major of the first *Nachtmusik*. The harmonic homeostasis of the whole symphony, the principal key, would accordingly be centered on C major, making the Seventh a C major symphony. In the overall plan the abrupt treatment of the keys corresponds to the unexpected events on the level of detail. It permits perspective relationships between the great tonal areas instead of the leveling transition, as in several places in the Eroica and Beethoven's Ninth Symphony, and many in Bruckner. Even the mature technique of the Sixth Symphony and *Das Lied von der Erde* often uses abrupt shifts to emphasize the plastic difference between harmonic levels, without fear of the static moment within a symphony. All compositional dimensions, including meter, tend toward deviation. In general, even numbers of measures predominate in Mahler. Agogic modifications, extensions, and abbreviations are nevertheless elaborated with delight, especially identical motives spun out to different lengths, doubled, or halved: the quantity of such performance-inspired nuances becomes the quality of the music itself.

Even the overall rhythm of Mahler's forms, the movement of the whole, is akin to the shift between major and minor, as earlier in Schubert to that between mourning and solace. There is exceptional evidence that this intention was in Mahler's mind. To the text of the bell chorus of the Third Symphony (in the *Wunderhorn* it bears the title "Armer Kinder Bettlerlied"[6] (poor children's begging song)—suppressed by Mahler but clandestinely all the more persistent—he has added something; in his texts, even the Klopstock resurrection hymn, "Wer hat denn dies Liedlein erdacht," and the Chinese texts for "Der Abschied," he intervenes in the same way as when altering repetitive song melodies. The passage[7] marked by Mahler *bitterlich*—a word, like *kläglich*, with a timbre that resonates dolefully in Mahler—"und sollt ich nicht weinen, du gütiger Gott," is answered by the sopranos, *ppp*, with shrill accents from the oboes, in Mahler's own words: "Du sollst ja nicht weinen! sollst ja nicht weinen." The mute will of music penetrates speech. Music addresses itself in words, as protest. The intention reappears solemnly in the Hymn of the Eighth Symphony, in the invocation of the Paraclete. But in turning to consolation music seeks less to express it than itself to console. This is always mingled in Mahler with a feeling of the futility of mere consolation. The protest is self-conscious: not without reason is the bell chorus of the Third thematically coupled to the Fourth Symphony, the absurd dream of a bleating and mournful solace. Mahler's music passes a maternal hand over the hair of those to whom it turns. So, in the *Kindertotenlieder*, tenderness for the nearest is intertwined with a doubtful solace for the most distant. The songs look on the dead as on children. The hope of the unrealized, which settles like a ray of holiness about those who die early, is not extinguished even for grownups. Mahler's music brings food to the mouth that is no more, watches over the sleep of those who shall never wake. If each of the dead resembles one who was murdered by the living, that person is also like one they ought to have rescued. "Oft denk ich, sie sind nur ausgegangen" (I think oft, they've only gone a journey)—not because they were children, but because stricken, uncomprehending love can comprehend death only as if the last going-out were that of homecoming children. In Mahler solace is the reflection of mourning. With trepidation, his music conserves in this reflection a soothing and healing virtue, the power to banish demons attributed by tradition to music since immemorial times, but which pales to a chimera with the disenchantment of the world. Asked as a child what he wanted to become, Mahler is said to have answered: a martyr. Because his music wishes most of all to be itself the Paraclete, it overtaxes itself and becomes inauthentic. This tinges its whole formal language. Just as solace dawns as a radiant "as if," Mahler speaks in indirect discourse. This as been noted from the first as his ironic or parodistic element. Schoenberg expresses the measure of truth contained in this somewhat vacuous and hostile observation:

His Ninth is most strange. In it, the author hardly speaks as an individual any longer. It almost seems as though this work must have a concealed author who used Mahler merely as his spokesman, as his mouthpiece.[8]

If the true composer is concealed, the manifest one is the conductor, who upholds the objectivity of the work against the fallible author. After that of Wagner, Mahler's is conductor's music of the highest rank, one that performs itself. The social standpoint of composition has so changed, has so contracted into itself, that it needs a medium interposed between the composer, who no longer simply communicates himself, and the subject matter, as in film the director becomes the conveyor of the material, eliminating the traditional author. In this intervening layer Mahler's brokenness is intertwined with historical problems of form. His persistence with symphonic objectivity at a time that no longer sanctioned symphonic form in the literal sense enforces the insertion of this mediating agency. The subject immanent in music, which informs the gesture of performance, reveals itself in the same way as the literary form of the story within a story. The enemy of all illusion, Mahler's music stresses its inauthenticity, underlines the fiction inherent in it, in order to be cured of the actual falsehood that art is starting to be. Thus what is perceived as an ironic character in Mahler springs from a force field located in form. Any fool can detect in his music traces of conductor's music, imitations of the familiar in the newly composed—but not the conductor's contribution to the formulations of the composer. It is the conductor's task to achieve a broken, inauthentic objectification at the expense of the spontaneous unity of music and composing subject. The supposedly natural source of the narrow stream of primary musical ideas is put into a more correct perspective by the conductor's knowledge of all of the possibilities from which he may choose. This knowledge imbues the process of composition with the technical deliberation ignorantly ascribed to Mahler's intellectuality. The conductor as composer has an ear not only for the sound but for the practice of the orchestra, the capabilities of the instruments as well as the exertions, weaknesses, exaggerations, and dullnesses that can be turned to his purposes. Borderline and exceptional situations, which the conductor studies through mistakes, extend his language, just as the experience of the orchestra as a living entity, correcting any static notion of sound, helps the music to produce itself spontaneously, to keep flowing. Orchestral *praxis*, a hard and unhappy fetter in the commercial sphere, releases Mahler's creative imagination. Underlying even this imagination's transcendental moments may be the primal movement of the conductor driving the orchestra on, as Speidel maintains in a review of Mahler's performance of the overture to *Lohengrin*. Wherever Mahler emphasizes characteristics running against the inclination of the music, his conducting manner must have been transferred to his composition. This makes his pieces less literal, as if they were as they are simply by nature. That Mahler was both a part of musical culture as a master saturated with its language, and yet separate from it, produces the specific atmosphere of his language. It is at once colloquial and that of a stranger. Its strangeness is heightened by the overfamiliar element, absent from compositions so deeply at one with their language that it changes dialectically with them. In Mahler the laconic and the concrete form a constellation recalling the German of Heine.[9] He cannot be charged with stylistic breaks since rupture is latent in his idea. As has often been asserted—and as he may well have stated himself— he harbored the stubborn notion of a bridge between popular and art music. He hoped for a collective hearing, without being prepared to sacrifice to it any degree of complexity or to negate the level of his own consciousness. Behind this stood, in objective musical terms, a need to strengthen melody, not for its own sake—in great symphonic works it was always secondary—but because the gigantic proportions of his movements, their claim to totality, to "world," would have been void without this substratum that has its history within them; synthesis would be idle without the diversity it synthesizes; it cannot become absolute without losing its meaning. But this need was no more satisfied by a popular music sunk into vulgarity than by all the advanced art-music of the age. Popular music was already a mirage of itself; this is why Mahler had to inject it with symphonic intensity. The fractured quality of his work expresses not least the impossibility of reconciling what has once diverged. The borrowings from the forms of folk song and popular music are endowed by the artistic language into which they have been transported with invisible quotation marks, and remain as sand in the mechanism of purely musical construction. The parade step of musical logic is disrupted by reflection on the social wrong that art-language irrevocably does to those denied the privilege of culture. The conflict between the high and the lower music in which, since the industrial revolution, the objective social process both of reification and of the disintegration of natural residues has been aesthetically reflected, and which no artistic will has pacified, is renewed in Mahler's music. His integrity decided in favor of high art. But the breach between the two spheres had become his special tone, that of brokenness. His music could properly be construed as a pseudomorph; aberrations are of its essence. In this he might be contrasted with Bruckner, with whom, as if mere length were a qualitative category, he is so heedlessly yoked together in Western countries. Mahler tracks down meaning in its absence, its absence in meaning. There is nothing of the kind in Bruckner; that much is true in the overbearing talk of his naïveté. Bruckner's formal language fractures precisely because he uses it intact. Even subjectivistic elements like Wagnerian enharmonic changes are converted back to the vocabulary of a precritical, dogmatic standpoint. What he desires on his own account is transferred unhesitatingly to the material, in which he resembles the much later composer Anton von Webern. Because the aesthetic subject has renounced its role as active shaper of the material, as had become the norm in the great music of the West, his work takes on the tone of something composed against the grain. The gradient of Bruckner's symphonies runs counter to the belief in composition as a subjective act of creation. Mahler's music, by contrast, is pseudomorphous through distancing itself from the objective medium of its vocabulary. It does this vocabulary violence in order to make it binding in a way the music itself finds problematic. A foreigner speaks music fluently, but as if with an accent. This was registered only by reactionary zealots; it was studiously ignored by the Schoenberg school, by way of protest, whereas it is only in the moment of inauthenticity, which unmasks the lie of authenticity, that Mahler has his truth. The pale or livid, murky or glaring light that the deviations throw on the musical language surrounding them prevents this language from being taken for granted; it is seen as if from outside. What is musically present becomes transparent. From inauthenticity the irreplaceable essence is distilled—a meaning that would remain absent if the particular were to be entirely and genuinely identical with itself. Objectively Mahler's music knows, and expresses the knowledge, that unity is attained not in spite of disjunction, but only through it.

What in Mahler sounds as if it were behind the times is bound up with the idea embodied in his work. His experiential core, brokenness, the musical subject's feeling of alienation, seeks to realize itself aesthetically by articulating the outward form not as immediate but as also broken, a cipher of the content, which is reciprocally influenced by the fractured form. In his work the musical phenomena are no more to be taken literally than the experiential core can directly become musical structure. If all of the other great music of the epoch withdrew into its native realm, borrowing nothing from a heteronomous reality or language, Mahler's music was innervated by the isolated, particular, impotently private element in such purity. In Mahler there resounds something collective, the movement of the masses, just as for seconds, in even the most trivial film, the force of the millions who identify themselves with it can be heard. Awesomely, Mahler's music makes itself the theater of collective energies. That in his later work he spurned the medium of chamber music, which must have appealed to one who could daily observe how much a composition is coarsened by the orchestral apparatus, bears witness to this. Mahler's music is the individual's dream of the irresistible collective. But at the same time it expresses objectively the impossibility of identification with it. Just as it knows of the nullity of the isolated ego that mistakenly believes itself absolute, so it also knows that this ego cannot aspire to being the collective subject directly. Mahler lacks all trace of the objectivist attitudes of the neo-Classicists who followed him; in those circles he was hated. His music neither speaks lyrically of the individual who expresses himself in it, nor inflates itself as the voice of the many; nor does it adopt simple language for their benefit. It derives its antinomous tension from the mutual unattainability of these poles.

Even when Mahler's symphonies project an echo of collective movements, they remain pseudomorphous through the voice of the subject speaking in solitude for those to whom it is drawn by hopeless
longing. If Mahler's music identifies itself with the masses, at the
same time it fears them. The extreme points of its collective urge, as
in the first movement of the Sixth Symphony, are the moments
when the blind and violent march of the many irrupts: moments of
trampling. That the Jew Mahler scented Fascism decades ahead, as
Kafka did in the piece on the synagogue, is no doubt the real source
of the despair of the wayfarer whom two blue eyes sent out into
the wide world ("Zwei blaue Augen" from *Lieder eines fahrenden
Gesellen*). Mahler relativizes the standpoint of the individual as the
corporeal bearer of music, without defecting to positive collectivism.
That too is one of the facets of his language. It is added as a further
aspect of his music, from the ruins of a collective either outmoded or
unattainable.[10] Meanwhile, this intention has spread to advanced
literature from Thornton Wilder to Eugene Ionesco. But where
Mahler's music does not itself appear as fractured, it must be
broken. It too is subject to Karl Kraus's dictum that a well-painted
gutter is worth more than a badly painted palace. This is conceded
by its development. Technical self-criticism gives way to self-
criticism of the idea. It takes us to the threshold of the intention of
advanced music: that composing has no chance of objectification,
that it can withstand social truth in no other way than if the composer, without peering beyond the aesthetic form of the composition, commits himself unconditionally to what is attainable within
his own situation.

During Mahler's lifetime, according to Schoenberg, a respected
critic charged his symphonies with being no more than "gigantic
symphonic pot-pourris."[11] Absurd as this may seem now that
Mahler's constructions have been recognized, it faithfully registers
what made them shocking. It was their irregular, unschematic aspect. Since Berlioz an irrationality in the procedure of composing
had shadowed the process of symphonic integration. In Mahler it is
no longer concealed, but at the same time reveals its own logic. Compared with Mahler's unschematic approach, the whole music of his

time, including the early Schoenberg, was traditional to the extent that it was expert. What is contemporary in Mahler is precisely the struggle with the expert. What in the potpourri was the necessity of indiscriminately assembling hackneyed melodies becomes in him the virtue of a structure that sensitively thaws the frozen groupings of accepted formal types. The coherence that they were supposed to guarantee is now founded on the fractured terseness of themes and forms, on the aspect assumed by the familiar that makes everything more than it merely is. This was prefigured in late-Romantic symphonic writing, above all that of the so-called national schools, in Tchaikovsky or Dvořák. The fictitiously popular specification of the themes places them so far in the foreground as to devalue the mediating categories of the classical tradition, where they invoke them, to theatrical claptrap or padding. What in them was involuntarily vulgar becomes in Mahler a provocative alliance with vulgar music. His symphonies shamelessly flaunt what rang in all ears, scraps of melody from great music, shallow popular songs, street ballads, hits. There are even adumbrations of songs that were only written much later, like the Maxim song in the First Symphony, or even, in the second movement of the Fifth, the Berlin "Wenn du meine Tante siehst" from the twenties. From the potpourri-like late Romantic pieces he takes over the striking and catchy individual coinages, but eliminates the trivialized connecting material. In its place he develops relationships concretely from the characters. Sometimes he lets these collide without transition, showing solidarity with Schoenberg's later criticism of mediation as something ornamental, superfluous. The potpourri satisfies more than one of Mahler's desiderata. It does not dictate to the composer what is to follow what; it demands no repeats, does not de-temporize time by a prescribed order of contents. It assists the decayed themes it accumulates to an afterlife in the second language of music. This Mahler prepares artificially. In his works the potpourri form, through the subterranean communication of its scattered elements, takes on a kind of instinctive, independent logic. Jacobinically the lower music irrupts into the higher. The complacent gloss of the intermediate form is demolished by the immoderate clamor from the military bandstands and palm court orchestras. Taste has as little authority for

Mahler as for Schoenberg.[12] Symphonic writing digs for the trea-
sure that only distant drum-rolls or vocal sounds promise, now that
music has set itself up as art. It seeks to stir the masses who have fled
culture music, yet without conforming to them. That the latter do
not easily follow symphonic organisms without crutches and so are
all the more ready to decry a lack of culture in them, was not allowed
for. But the conclusion will have been drawn that the disparate
levels are not to be reunited by decree. The unrisen lower is stirred
as yeast into high music. The rude vigor and immediacy of a musical
entity that can neither be replaced nor forgotten: the power of nam-
ing[13] is often better protected in kitsch and vulgar music than in a
high music that even before the age of radical construction had sacrificed all that to the principle of stylization. This power is mobilized
by Mahler. Free as only one can be who has not himself been entirely swallowed by culture, in his musical vagrancy he picks up the
broken glass by the roadside and holds it up to the sun so that all the
colors are refracted.

> That he of all people, who has no material wants—the "bar-
> barian," as we often called him because of his distaste for lux-
> ury and comfort and the beautiful things of life—that he
> should be surrounded by such splendour seems to him such an
> irony of fate that it often brings an involuntary smile to his
> lips.[14]

In the debased and vilified materials of music he scratches for illicit
joys. He takes pity on the lost, that it should not be forgotten and
should be grafted to the good form that will preserve it from sterile
resemblance to itself. How ingeniously he gathers up the heteronomous, the dregs for the autonomous structure, is attested by the
scandalously audacious posthorn solo in the Third Symphony. In it
Mahler elaborates the subjective rudiment, the player's rubato.
Fanfare and song intermingle: the entry of the song proper[15] ensues
with the dominant chord, as if, inaudibly, a part of the melody had
preceded it; the stretching out of the playing changes the melody
here too, rescuing it from a trivial eight-measure pattern. The harmony is imperceptibly expressive. If banality is the essence of
musical reification, it is both preserved and redeemed by the in-

spired, improvising voice that animates the concrete. Thus the music incorporates even the fracture without which the whole would disintegrate. But at the second entry of the posthorn the violins, in Mahler's score direction (*wie nachhorchend*), are "listening for it,"[16] as if they were shaking their heads. By reflecting the rejection of the music by taste as impossible, as kitsch, they affirm the possible, the promise without which breath could not for a second be drawn.

Mahler inferred the revolt against bourgeois music from that very music. Since Haydn it has communicated a plebeian element. It rumbles in Beethoven, while Faust on the Easter Sunday walk with his pedantic amanuensis speaks for that stratum as if it were nature. The emancipation of the bourgeois class found its musical echo. But it was no more identical aesthetically than in reality with the humanity it proclaimed. Humanity is restricted by the class relationship. That it is withheld from those of formally equal rights makes their attitude rebellious. The bourgeois are plebeian as long as their autonomous spirit is not universally realized. In the artwork too: ill-dressed, unmannerly people romp in a ceremonial chamber, the absolutistic imago of which bourgeois music continues to delineate. With the consolidation of the bourgeoisie the plebeian element had been gradually toned down to a folkloristic charm. In Mahler, in a phase when the crushing reality could no longer be placated through metaphor by the aesthetic sensorium, that unruly noise grows shrill. What bourgeois taste had earlier savored as red blood cells for its own regeneration now threatens its life. Beethoven had still been able to reconcile the plebeian element with the classical in relation to a diversity that is worked on as "material" but nowhere obtrudes autonomously, unvarnished. But Mahler's time no longer knew a common people that could be seen as as bucolic, and from which musical play-acting might decently have borrowed its costume. No more did the technical level by now attained by music allow the plebeian to be absorbed. For this reason the lowly in Mahler does not embody the elemental or the mythic, nothing of primal nature, even when his music evokes such associations, as in the moods of the cowbells; there music is pausing to draw breath, knowing the way back to be blocked, rather than feigning to follow that way. Fruitless to search for anti-mind in Mahler. Rather, the lowly is for him the negative of a culture that has aborted. Form, measure, taste, finally that autonomy of structure that even his symphonies pursued are marked by the guilt of those who exclude the others from them. What makes art-works a closed structure of meaning—the aura that seals them from the degradation of reality, their fastidious refinement—is not just socially based on material control and the culture arising from it, but carries the privilege of noli me tangere into its innermost sanctum. The spirit that in great music celebrates itself the more tyrannically the greater the music is, despises the base physical work of the others. Mahler's music will not play according to these rules. Desperately it draws to itself what culture has spurned, as wretched, injured, and mutilated as culture hands it over. The art-work, chained to culture, seeks to burst the chain and show compassion for the derelict residue; in Mahler each measure is an opening of arms. But what the norm of culture has rejected, the Freudian leavings of the phenomenal world, does not, according to this symphonic writing, exhaust itself in complicity with culture: Freud's doctrine of a connivance of id and superego against the ego is tailor-made for Mahler. The residue is to drive the art-work beyond the appearance it has become under culture, and reinstate something of the corporeality by which music, insofar as its play represents nothing, is distinguished from other aesthetic media. Through the lower as a social category, Mahler's music intends to transcend mind as ideology. The first draft of the theme "Alles Vergängliche ist nur ein Gleichnis" from the Eighth Symphony, kept for decades in the house of Alban Berg, is on a piece of toilet paper. The hidden impulse of his music seeks to liquidate the superstructure and penetrate to what the immanence of musical culture conceals. But art is no more capable of this than is any form of truth as pure immediacy. Unseduced by the romanticism of authenticity and essence, Mahler never pretends to show that naked state of being unmetaphorically, as something existent. Hence the brokenness. What in Beethoven still masquerades as jest—the birds at the end of the scene by the brook grinding like mechanical toys; the involuntarily comic aspect of the primeval symbols in Wagner's Ring—becomes the a priori form of all that in

Mahler's music is called nature. Only awareness of this protects Mahler from that enthusiasm that from his beginnings was summed up by the dreadful word "cosmic," and that deserves the scorn poured on the intellectual who passes solemn hours of contemplation in high pastures. Unlike Stravinsky, however, Mahler does not deride his infantile models. The standpoint of his music toward objectivity is far from malicious archaicizing. He vents his ire neither on the powerless old nor on the impotent subject. In his much-quoted ironic moments the subject complains of the futility of its own exertions instead of mocking the lost and charmed world of images. Mahler is never satisfied by such moments. The subject, descending from the superstructure, tears up and changes what it encounters. If, at the risk of ready misunderstanding, one attempted to compare Mahler and Stravinsky with trends in psychology, Stravinsky would be on the side of the Jungian archetypes, while the Enlightenment consciousness of Mahler's music recalls the cathartic method of the Freud who, a German-Bohemian Jew like Mahler and encountering the latter at a critical point in his life, declined to cure his person out of respect for his work, and so showed himself entirely superior to those of his followers who dispose of Baudelaire by diagnosing his mother complex. In Mahler the composing subject does not attach itself to the infantile stratum, but admits it in order to demythologize it. After the destruction of a musical culture debased to ideology, a second whole is shored up from the fragments and scraps of memory. In it the subjective organizing power allows the return of culture, which art opposes but cannot eradicate. Each Mahlerian symphony asks how, from the ruins of the musical objective world, a living totality can arise. Not despite the kitsch to which it is drawn is Mahler's music great, but because its construction unties the tongue of kitsch, unfetters the longing that is merely exploited by the commerce that the kitsch serves. The development of Mahler's symphonic movements sketches salvation by means of dehumanization.

3

Mahler's way of proceeding is guided not by traditional principles of form, but by the specific musical content and his conception of the overall progression of each piece. However, essential genres in his idea of form are: breakthrough (*Durchbruch*), suspension (*Suspension*), and fulfillment (*Erfüllung*). Passages embodying "breakthrough" are those mentioned in the First Symphony, and later the moment in the second movement of the Fifth where the wind instruments change direction into D major. Suspensions compose out the old *senza tempo* within the main progression as against "extraterritorial" parts: from the "Bird of Death" passage before the entry of the chorus in the Second, the posthorn episode in the Third, the episodes in the development sections of the first movements of the Sixth and Seventh, to the measures evoking spring in "Der Trunkene" in *Das Lied von der Erde*, and the passage marked *Etwas gehalten* (somewhat restrained) in the Burlesque of the Ninth. Mahlerian suspensions tend to be sedimented as episodes. These are essential to him: roundabout ways that turn out retrospectively to be the direct ones. Among the codified formal categories, Mahler's concept of fulfillment comes closest to the *Abgesang* of bar form, rehearsed for his generation by *Die Meistersinger.* Examples of fulfillment as *Abgesang* are the short close of the exposition in the first movement of the Third or the end of the recapitulation in the Finale of the Sixth, before the introduction appears for the last time, and the third stanza of the first movement of *Das Lied von der Erde*. The reason why, until its renaissance in Wagner, the *Abgesang* was hardly used throughout the whole *basso continuo* era is probably that, being the fulfillment of a musical context by something fundamentally new, it collided with the idea of the intrinsic closedness of modern music, the economic principle of which derives everything like interest from a basic stock. Mahler's revolt against such parsimony remembered the *Abgesang* independently of historical instruction. What in Mahler's symphonic writing is not inherent in the form, not calculable, becomes itself, as *Abgesang*, a formal category, unlike and identical at once. The inauthentic gropes toward the In-itself (*An sich*), toward what the individual themes, ascetically resisting the subjective demand that all should be derived from within themselves, have left room for. Archaic remnants within popular music, above all in the march, may have induced Mahler to reconstruct the *Abgesang*. Its model in physical movement is the sequence of "Mark time" and "Forward march." Accumulated power is unleashed. Fulfillment is unfettering, the physical pattern of freedom. Its type also includes, without *Abgesang* function, the beginning of the recapitulation in the first movement of the Eighth, the fortissimo repeat of the main theme early in the first movement of the Ninth, and a great deal in the Finale of the Sixth, even the end of the second theme group in its exposition. Yet it is not only such formal elements that are fulfilled in Mahler; the idea of fulfillment is at work throughout the whole symphonic structure. Everywhere the obligation of expectation is honored. Music reaps fulfillment as gain when it abstains from dramatic plot thickenings or momentary accounting. Mahler could find fulfillment fields in early Brahms: in the first movement of the G Major Piano Quartet, or the march episode in its Andante. The history of nineteenth-century music—to the extent that it focused on semitonal movement and chromatic coloring—vastly increased tension and devalued relaxation. This gave rise to a technical disproportion, a certain denial of content. Both were reinforced as the conventional means for simulating fulfillment, above all the return to the main key, grew increasingly inadequate in face of the increasing tensions. Mahler undoubtedly remained true to diatonicism not least because he wanted to resolve the tensions more energetically than the means of *Tristan* permitted. But as he could no longer rely simply on tonality, fulfillments became for him a task of the purely musical form. Where colons or question marks are composed, they cannot be answered by mere punctuation marks but always by a sentence. The actual energy of the characters can never be less than the potential energy of the tension: the music says, in a sense, *voilà*. This element was inherited by Schoenberg, whose dictum that music theory is always concerned with the beginning and end and never with the decisive events between alludes to this state of affairs. His idea of the resolution of tension through the dynamic essence of form is the self-consciousness of a Mahlerian need. Justice holds sway in the technique of composition. But not only measure for measure. The permanent concern for fulfillment summons the unexchangeable to the heart of the composer's procedure, instead of leaving it outside as an abstract wishful image or a poeticizing vision. Breakthrough is always suspension, that of the immanent context; but not every suspension is a breakthrough. That it had the necessary strength Mahler came to doubt; after the Fifth his movements hardly risk the notion of transcendence as a new immediacy. Involuntarily his musical logic has aligned itself with the philosophical one, whereby it is impossible to leap from the dialectic into the unconditional without danger of lapsing into the wholly conditional; he shrinks as a composer from invoking the name of God in order not to deliver Him up to His adversary. The intention of the breakthrough is gradually mediatized. The suspensions give notice to formal immanence without positively asserting the presence of the Other; they are self-reflections of what is entangled in itself, no longer allegories of the absolute. Retrospectively they are caught up by the form from whose elements they are composed. Mahler's fulfillment fields achieve by form, by their relation to what preceded them, what the breakthrough promised itself from outside, and what the symphonic-dramatic type reserved to the explosion of the moment. In Mahler the breakthrough is momentary; the suspensions stretch themselves out, fulfillments are thematic forms of a specific nature. But because Mahler's music keeps the promise, because it is truly consummated where other music, as Busoni observed, attains its climaxes and then, disappointed and disappointing, starts again from below, a yearning is fulfilled with which the unfettered spirit really approaches all music and to which the fettered one only believes itself superior as taste because it has again and again been cheated of it, and most of all in the greatest works of art. The aversion to kitsch is repelled by its claim to be the awaited, which its deficiencies debase. Kitsch hoaxes with what, at the same time, it has that art lacks. Mahler seeks to eliminate this false choice by divesting kitsch of what high music denies while curing it of fraud by that trait of high music to which alone fulfillment is truly granted. If Mahler takes leave of the glorious moment, it leaves him spaces of lasting present. In his fulfillment passages abides what otherwise flees, as happens before him perhaps only occasionally in Bruckner: the F-sharp major middle passage of the Adagio in the latter's Seventh Symphony. The G major episode, formed from an inconspicuous counterpoint to the main theme complex, following the exposition of the first movement of Mahler's Fourth Symphony, a blissful passage, lies before the listener like a village before which he is seized by the feeling that this might be what he seeks.[1] That music becomes capable of such duration compensates for the abandonment of the authentically symphonic principle. Mahler's sense of form demands, however, that this episodic character of the whole symphony should not be lost again; the spun-out first theme of the variation movement in the Fourth, free of all strident pathos, has the same contented homeland peace, healed of the pain of frontiers. Its authenticity, which need not fear that of Beethoven, passes the test in the sense that longing rests, yet sounds incorruptibly again in the *klagend* (lamenting) second theme, with its *singend* (singing) transcendent consequent.[2]

Mahlerian categories like suspension or fulfillment suggest an idea that could contribute, beyond the scope of his work, to endowing music with speech through theory: the idea of a material theory of form, the deduction of formal categories from their meaning. This is neglected by academic theory of form, which operates with abstract classifications such as first theme, transition, second or closing theme, without understanding these divisions in terms of their functions. In Mahler the usual abstract formal categories are overlaid with material ones; sometimes the former become specifi-

cally the bearer of meaning; sometimes material formal principles
are constituted beside or below the abstract ones, which, while continuing to provide the framework and to support the unity, no
longer themselves supply a connection in terms of musical meaning. Mahler's material formal categories become especially clear
physiognomically when the music falls inwards as in a kaleidoscope.
The end of the development in the first movement of the Ninth
Symphony, for example, gives the impression, in the words of Erwin Ratz, of "a terrifying collapse."[3] The traditional theory of form
is acquainted, usually in the closing section before the coda, with
fields of disintegration. In them the thematic contours dissolve in a
play of tones, for example on the dominant, which operates more or
less like a formula; not unusual, too, are diminuendi elaborated over
relatively long stretches. The collapsing passages in Mahler, however, no longer merely mediate between others or conclude elaborations, but speak for themselves. While they are embedded in the
overall progression of the form, at the same time they extend
through it as something in their own right: negative fulfillment. If
what the elaboration has promised takes place in the fulfillment
fields, in the collapses there is enacted what the musical process
fears. They do not merely modify the composition, which has become less dense in them or has been entirely dispersed. They are
formal entities as characters. A material theory of forms would always deal in Mahler with formal sections that, instead of being filled
with characters, are by their nature formulated as characters. The
category of collapse can be traced back to a very early and simple
model, the close of the third song of *Lieder eines fahrenden
Gesellen*: "Ich wollt', ich läg' auf der schwarzen Bahr," where, over
a dominant pedal, a series of parallel chords tumbles in descent.
They are not a transition to something else; they are themselves the
goal, the fragments of motives after them merely a coda, the final
song an epilogue. Mahler took over this type unmistakably in the
first movement of the Second Symphony,[4] which generally shows
the collapsing tendency. Such a collapse is composed with full mastery in the Funeral March of the Fifth Symphony.[5] It dynamizes the
form, yet without the traditional formal departments being simply
abolished by elaboration; rather, the dynamics of the catastrophe

section are themselves also a character, a quasi-spatial field. Not only do the collapse sections meet a formal requirement of relaxation, they decide the content of the music by the character elaborated in them.

Mahler's characters, taken together, make up a world of images. At first glance it seems Romantic, whether in a rural or small-town sense, as if the musical cosmos were warming itself by an irretrievable social one: as if the unstilled longing were projected backwards. That Mahler was nevertheless proof against Spitzweg and the pseudo-Gothic, his flight of imagination extending the idyll, on the model of the Wagnerian mastersinger, into a plan for a dynamic whole, was made possible only by the brokenness of his images. Conversely, the images are also broken by the symphonic tendency, the totality of which obliterates the immediacy of details. In the poems with which Mahler's music is steeped, those of the *Wunderhorn*, the Middle Ages and the German Renaissance were themselves already derivatives, as if printed on broadsheets telling of noble knights that are yet halfway to being newspapers. Mahler's affinity with his texts lay less in the illusion of coziness than in a premonition of unaltered, savage times that overtook him in his ordered late-bourgeois existence, perhaps motivated by the indigence of his youth. To his mistrust of the peace of the imperialist era war is the normal state, and human beings are pressganged soldiers. He pleads musically for peasant cunning against the overlords, for those who desert their marriages, for outsiders, the persecuted and incarcerated, starving children, forlorn hopes. The term socialist realism would fit only Mahler if it were not so depraved by domination; often the Russian composers of around 1960 sound like vandalized Mahler. Berg is the legitimate heir of this spirit; in the *Ländler* in *Wozzeck*, which urges the poor folk into an ungainly, subservient dance, is mingled a clarinet rhythm from the Scherzo of the Fourth Symphony. The prevalent ideology of the true, beautiful, and good, with which Mahler's music first made common cause, is inverted into valid protest. Mahler's humanity is a mass of the disinherited. Even the late works refuse to sell off the materialistic element: the disillusionment in which they terminate answers the historical woe whose furrows Mahler's music discerns on the face of a past that is yet worth singing and telling. Mahler's Romanticism negates itself through disenchantment, mourning, long remembrance. But his world of images, even as that of his own day, is historical, a farewell to the enclaves of traditional, pre-capitalist Europe that still lingered in the late industrial phase and which, condemned by development, glows with a reflected joy that was never present as long as the simple commodity economy was the dominant form of production. Mahler's old-German images are as much dream wishes of the period about 1900. The motto to the second *Nachtmusik* in the Seventh Symphony could be furnished by verses such as Rilke's "The chiming clocks call each to each, and one sees to the floor of time." The volume in which they are found is called the "Book of Images." They were ephemeral enough, and a trace of their sentimentality impairs even Mahler's image-world. However, his music transcends their dimensions in that it is not, as in the contemplation of essences of the contemporary phenomenology, for example, becalmed by the images, but constrains them to a movement that is finally that of the history that rapt immersion in the images would so gladly forget.

Colorfully different, the images engage in protean intermingling. Their transformations are supervised by extreme precision of composition. Each phenomenon, from a whole symphonic movement down to an individual phrase, to a motive and its transformation, produces exactly the effect intended: the New Music, particularly Berg, copied him in this. Elaborations seem to say: this is an elaboration; interruptions occur with unmistakable abruptness; if the music opens up, one hears colons; if it is fulfilled, the line noticeably exceeds the preceding intensity and does not depart from the level now attained. Resolutions clearly blur the contours and the sound. Marcato underlines the essential, announces: "Here I am"; a following passage is demonstrated by fragments of earlier motives, a picking up by harmonic continuation; what is to be entirely different and appear new is really that. Such precision makes the characters emerge clearly: they coincide with their emphatic formal function, the *characteristica universalis* of Mahler's music. The rule of clarity to which he rigorously subjected the instrumentation in particular resulted from his reflection as a composer: the less the music is articulated by tonal language, the more strictly must it ensure its own articulation. For this reason it calls its forms, as it were, by their names, composes their types as Schoenberg's wind quintets did paradigmatically later;[6] the imaginary Adrian Leverkühn, who receives more from Mahler than the high G on the cellos from the end of the first *Nachtmusik* in the Seventh Symphony, raised this principle to the canon of his works. Mahler's lack of naïveté in relation to his own language has its technical correlative in elucidation. What characterizes is, for that very reason, no longer simply what it is, but, as the word *character* intends, a sign. Mahler drew his functional characters—what each individual part contributes to the form—from the stock of traditional music. But they are used autonomously, without regard to their place in the established pattern. He can therefore invent melodies that clearly have the character of sequels, essences of the closing themes of sonata form; of such kind, for example, is the *Abgesang* figure in the Adagietto of the Fifth Symphony.[7] Its character derives, no doubt, from its drawn-out beginning, a hesitation that checks the flow of time and disposes the music to retrospection. Essential to such closing models is the descending second, an interval for which Mahler had a general predilection. It imitates the falling voice, melancholy like the speaker whose endings fall. Without the intrusion of meanings, a linguistic gesture is transferred to music. Of course, something as commonplace as the descending second only functions as a gesture when accentuated; the Adagietto has been rich in descending seconds previously, but only through their lengthening in the *Abgesang* do they become something special. In general Mahler's music inclines to the descending. Devotedly it accedes to the gravitational slope of musical language. Yet as Mahler expressly assimilates this gradient, it becomes colored with expressive values that it otherwise lacked in a tonal context. This contrasts Mahler with Bruckner. The differences of inflection stand for diverging intentions, Bruckner's affirmation and Mahler's discovery of solace in unrelieved mourning. However, the Mahlerian characters seldom inform the individual figures as purely as in this *Abgesang*. Usually they are also determined by their relation to what has preceded

them. The chromatically descending closing theme in the first
movement of the Second Symphony only has its effect of crushed
calm (*zögernd*) after the violent outburst.[8]

Into the characteristic detail seeps back the meaning that vanished with the ritual execution of the whole. Nevertheless, the music does not therefore find its peace in details that, though charged,
are merely accumulated and mutually indifferent. Rather, the less
the form is substantially prescribed, the more insistently it is sought
by compositions that begin with the unprotected individual figure.
The whole, once the a priori ground of the composition, becomes the
task of each Mahlerian movement. Form itself is to become characteristic, an event. This question had grown to prominence within
the tradition. Symphonic flow was the music's ability to gain momentum, as, above all, in Beethoven's developments. Mahler too
does not lack it; it is magnificently in evidence in some passages of
the waltz complex of the Scherzo of the Ninth Symphony, though
its first presentation was static.[9] But Mahler's movements, in their
entirety, are streams on which is borne whatever is caught in them,
yet without its particularity being entirely absorbed. They cannot
cause the characteristic to disappear because they recognize no
structure beyond the configuration of the characteristic. Such concern for the whole is Mahler's antithesis to late Romanticism, which
took its pride in the mere characteristic of the particular and so degraded it to a commodity. Even when the young Mahler writes
genre-like pieces in the manner of the time, they vibrate with the
whole; even what takes delight in limitation seeks to be rid of its
own limits. In the well-ordered groups of the first movement of the
Fifth dynamic passages are inserted, as in the section leading back
after the first trio.[10] The fanfare, on its first return in the exposition
of the March, plunges seething into a mass that hisses with a clash of
cymbals.[11] So a lament opposed to discipline is set at liberty amid
the somewhat static planes of a stylized military march. In Mahler
the lyrical subject is painfully divested, by the formal sequence that
it initiates, of its mere individuality. The part and the whole do not
harmonize as in Viennese classicism. Their relationship is aporetic.
The impetus of the totality must relativize the individual in order to
be felt; the details should not comply conciliatingly with it if they

are not to lose the character which alone fits them to the whole; for all their particularity they remain, in relation to the idea of a totality, essentially incomplete. Mahler's way of mastering aporia constitutes his achievement as a composer. Either he experiments with the particular until it finally becomes a whole. Or he studiously, artistically avoids rounded completeness: then its absence becomes a negative meaning. Or he secretly stamps the individual, irregular part that sounds like a passing idea passively received by the total composition in such a way that it is not simply there, is not something definitive to be "accepted," but strains beyond itself and its limited thusness (*Sosein*). Binding yet non-obligatory individual formulations, the renunciation of fixed themes, is the pre-eminent means. Subjectivity, which in Mahler seems to relinquish its substance to the objective, still penetrates the latter—this sets the limit to his objectivist intention. The plastic cantabile models derived from song melodies nevertheless are nowhere self-sufficient. The old dynamic of symphonic composition has taken possession of the emancipated details. Sometimes they pass over into the Other, sometimes they demand it as a foil; sometimes they split up as the resolution fields once did in classicism. To this extent Mahler's music resists academic formalism no less than the flat association of particulars of the New German school. The aim is an objective whole that neither forfeits a part of subjective differentiation nor attains its objectivity by surreptitious means.

For this reason the limited stock of types available from great music was inadequate to Mahler's need for universal characterization. Through the unqualified primacy of the whole over the parts in Viennese classicism, the figures in that music frequently resembled each other and converged. They shunned extreme contrast, without which the Mahlerian whole would not be formed. He looks for support not only in declining late Romanticism, but above all in vulgar music. This offers him crude stimulants that the selective taste of higher music has rejected, like the "thrilling" effects of military bands. One seems to have heard the passage with trills in the allegro exposition of the Finale of the Sixth Symphony[12] innumerable times in marches. But through the context in which these piercing trills are played they take on a gruesomely unmetaphorical tone undreamed of in their normal habitat. This deadly, unstylized quality is of the nature of Mahlerian characters: joy is indeed, and not only in him, hardly a character. Where the young Mahler sets out to compose contentedly in unbroken Austrian, as in the Andante of the Second Symphony, he verges on complacency, and later in the Adagietto on shallow sentimentality; the music of the mature Mahler knows happiness only as something revocable, as in the iridescent solo violin episode in the recapitulation of the Finale of the Sixth Symphony;[13] "Der Trunkene im Frühling" is jubilant in the manner that Wagner discovered for composition at the end of the first act of *Tristan:* "O Wonne voller Tücke! O Trug-geweihtes Glücke!".[14] Characterization, the objectivation of the expressive, is intimately bound up with suffering. Its painful element in the late works astringently permeates the whole complexion of Mahler's work. His tonal, predominantly consonant music sometimes has the climate of absolute dissonance, the blackness of the New Music. Sometimes the characters of outbreak and gloom become one in a tone of panic wildness; aside from the first trio from the Funeral March in the Fifth and much in the Sixth, the power of the musical stream, its whirling into a vortex of terror, is potentiated above all in the development of the Third; the composition becomes disproportionate to the human body. The outbreak, from the place it has escaped from, appears as savage: the anti-civilizational impulse as musical character. Such moments evoke the doctrine of Jewish mysticism that interprets evil and destructiveness as scattered manifestations of the dismembered divine power; all in all, the Mahlerian traits to which the cliché of pantheistic belief has been crudely applied are more likely to originate in a subterranean mystical stratum than in portentous monistic natural religion. This might illuminate the observation advanced hesitantly by Guido Adler as "paradoxical," that monotheistic and pantheistic aspects intersect in Mahler.[15]

Characterization in Mahler's acoustic material extends to the physiognomies of instruments that leap untamed from the tutti: the emancipated, disequilibrating trombones in the first movement of the Third Symphony; echoing, booming drum motives in the first *Nachtmusik* and the Scherzo of the Seventh, and even of the Sixth.

In Mahler's orchestra the balance that was still maintained in Wagner is upset for the first time, despite all the increase in color as compared to classicism. The the individual voice is clarified at the expense of the total sound. In the Finale of the First Symphony laceration is intensified beyond all mediating measure into a totality of despair, behind which, to be sure, the nonchalant triumphal close pales to an affair of mere management. The closed surface of sound is disrupted in a new music with traditional means. Between academic failure and aesthetic success there is as little distinction here as in every significant work of art. The genius of Mahler's sense of form is manifested when, in the midst of the ravaged total situation, he places an inordinately long and intense, unbroken upper-voice melody, as if that state needed the other extreme, a self-contained part that makes itself independent of the whole, and which begins to glow in its surroundings, which cannot contain it. The same instinct that commands Mahler to contrast the unbroken to the atomized then forbids him, against the pattern of the sonata and rondo, to repeat the D-flat major melody, the structure of which is unique. It appears merely as a fragment, in the whirl of atoms. Through its annihilation it is incorporated after all; following such destruction it could not come independently a second time. Mahler treats form unschematically not from the mere inclination of an innovator, but from the realization that musical time, unlike architecture, permits no simple relationships of symmetry. To it like is unlike, unlikeness may be the basis of likeness; nothing is unaffected by succession. What happens must always take specific account of what happened before. The First Symphony, in which Mahler does not take issue with the weight of tradition, is especially rich in anti-formalist characters. It hurls unmediated contrasts to the point of ambivalence between mourning and mockery. The potpourri of the third movement admits defeat by the world's course, which it despairs to overcome, and coordinates irreconcilables, both quite early on[16] and, above all, at the sudden acceleration.[17]

The extreme example of the character symphony is the Fourth. Its totality, entirely broken, is produced by the need for characterization, the whole being character as much as its elements. It is subject to a law of diminution. Its image-world is that of childhood. The means are reduced, without heavy brass; horns and trumpets are more modest in number. No father figures are admitted to its precincts. The sound avoids all monumentality, which had attached itself to the symphonic idea since Beethoven's Ninth. The instrumental art of characterization takes advantage of this asceticism: the soloistically intimate colors, the melodious, un-fanfarelike voices produced by the horns in the Fourth as softer and darker substitutes for the bass winds are unexampled even in *Die Meistersinger*. The need to elicit the most varied colors from a smaller palette results in new combinations like the muted gloom of low horns and bassoons in the second movement, new timbres like the transparency of the clarinets in the last. The unison of the four flutes in the development[18] does not just reinforce the sound. It creates an effect sui generis, that of a dream ocarina: such must have been children's instruments that no one ever heard. The reduction of the orchestra caused the symphonic writing to approach chamber-music procedures, to which Mahler, after the alfresco quality of the first three symphonies, returned again and again, most markedly in the *Kindertotenlieder*, which are quoted in the variations movement of the Fourth.[19] However, no more than the last *Kindertotenlied* does the Fourth Symphony remain chamber music. Whenever it wishes it creates massive tutti effects, to which the chamber complexes are joined as an element. They too are functions of the composition, the movement: they irradiate the subtle, constantly modified weft of voices. This not only contrasts with the broad brush strokes, but leads toward them through condensation. At the climax at the end of the development the solemn fanfare of the Fifth is heard.[20] According to a statement attributed to Mahler, it was supposed to lead the development, which, in Schumann's sense, deported itself "almost too earnestly," back to order and play; with a gesture of Viennese skepticism, all that was reduced to nothing. Through this passage the four first symphonies are bracketed with the purely instrumental middle ones. All of Mahler's works communicate subterraneanly, like Kafka's through the passages of his Burrow. No work of his is so thoroughly a work that it becomes a monad vis-à-vis the others. The mastery that he attained in the economy of the Fourth and retrospectively transferred to the image-world of the so-called *Wunderhorn* symphonies informs every measure. In the Fourth Symphony he writes counterpoint for the first time in earnest, although polyphony did not dominate the imagination of the earlier pieces. The counterpoint seeks to restore the intensity of texture that might have been diminished by the sacrifice of the heavy brass. But the contrapuntal elements also characterize. In the first complex of themes in the first movement a clarinet and bassoon figure is improvised,[21] enveloped by the strings but, in a correct performance, not to be overheard. Through the interval of a ninth, which comes into the foreground in the false recapitulation after the end of the exposition, the figure gradually assumes the equal rights of a main theme, which the formally correct structure first denied it. The huge interval, from *d* to *b'*, to which the contrapuntal theme seems to reach out from the first, is only fittingly taken up by the cellos in the false recapitulation.[22] Mahler's ability to manage large-scale symphonic structures is such that a tension is latently felt over many sections within a movement and is only resolved when the pattern returns. The treatment of form is no less spontaneous. At the climax of the first movement an intentionally infantile, noisily cheerful field[23] is presented, the forte growing increasingly uncomfortable until the retransition with the fanfare. But with utmost speed, and offending all the formal rules, it is repeated in the recapitulation,[24] instead of the original transition.[25] This has a precise formal purpose. For the noisy passage is related through motives to the earlier transition—or, if one will, to the *Abgesang* of the main theme. Yet if the passage returned in its first form, it would fall short of its modification in the first fanfare-like noise-field. A fanfare cannot be further developed, only repeated, as if the music were manically obsessed by the thought of outbreak. It therefore here prefers to make do with an identity which, though primitive and premature, is striking through its irregularity, than to warm up something more distant or once more set in motion a dynamic in the recapitulation that would only duplicate in vain the very extensive one in the development. After the development, at the dictate of the fanfare, has dwindled away, masking the beginning of the recapitulation, the music is swept from the scene by a general pause, until suddenly[26] the main theme continues from the middle of its restatement;[27] this moment is like the child's joy at being abruptly transported from the forest to the old-fashioned market place of Miltenberg. Haydn's joke in the Toy Symphony is widened in the Fourth into a spacious fantasy realm in which everything seems to happen once again. Like the noise-field, children make a din when they batter pans and possibly break them. The destructive urge, which lurks malevolently behind all triumphal music and shames it, is absolved as unrationalized play. The entire Fourth Symphony shuffles nonexistent children's songs together; to it the golden book of song is the book of life. The sound of the great drum in it is as drums once seemed before the age of seven; the symphony is a solitary attempt at musical communication with the déjà vu, in genuine color like the imago of the gypsy wagon and the ship's cabin. Mahler discovered the symphony, too, in the marches that his ear, forgetting everything, pursued like children running after the tinkling of triangle and bell tree (*Schellenbaum*). The sound of a band is to the musical sensorium of the child much like brightly colored railroad tickets to its optical sense, scintillating against the commonplace gray, the last trace of a world of perception not yet confiscated by commerce. Not lacking among the children's images in Mahler's music are the vanishing snatches from musical processions, flashing far off and promising more than they ever fulfill in deafening closeness; involuntarily remembered, the once coercive marches sound in Mahler like dreams of undiminished freedom. The adaptation of marches was made easier because, although belonging to the lower music denigrated by culture, they had at their disposal a canon of procedures, a relatively highly developed formal language, the suggestive power of which was not as remote from that of the symphony as cultural arrogance assumed. As later with jazz, in the nineteenth century a certain type of artistically unassuming but technically qualified musician is likely to have gone into military music and found there a collective undercurrent of very exact musical forms; this may have been what Mahler admired in marches. But whoever claims ownership of marches, as once of

his lead soldiers, to him the door opens on the irrevocable. The en-
trée is hardly cheaper than death. Like Euridice, Mahler's music has
been abducted from the realm of the dead. Not only in the second
movement of the Fourth are the images of the child and death superimposed. If the language one understood as a child dawns across
the aeons, the joy of speaking it again is chained to the loss of in-
dividuation. Children who could hardly correctly grasp Mahler's
complex and many-layered music may yet in their error have better understood the blissful pain of songs like "Ich ging mit Lust
durch einen grünen Wald" than the grownups. By cooking their
musical fare Mahler takes on himself precipitously the historical
process of the regression of hearing. Consolingly he hastens to
succor an ego-enfeebled humanity incapable of autonomy or synthesis. He simulates disintegrating language in order to lay bare
the potential of what would be better than the proud values of
culture.

Nowhere is Mahler's music more pseudomorphous than in the
seraphic symphony. The bells in the first measure that very softly
tinge the eighth notes in the flute have always shocked the normal
listener, who feels he is being played for a fool. They really are fool's
bells, which, without saying it, say: none of what you now hear is
true. A passage from the text of the *Wunderhorn* song "Der Schildwache Nachtlied," in the magnificently dissonant middle section of
arching wide-spanned intervals, runs: "An Gottes Segen ist alles
gelegen! Wer's glauben tut! Wer's glauben tut!"[28] ("God's grace
takes care of everything. Who believes that? Who believes that?")
—which comments on the image of blessedness with which the
symphony ends. It paints paradise in rustic anthropomorphous
colors to give notice that it does not exist. The unbelief that under-
lies Christianity in all the converted countries that it has subjected,
and in which remnants of mythical nature religion mingle impen-
etrably with beginnings of Enlightenment, makes its entrance in
musical images of faith. The fool's bells have their musical consequence at once. The main theme, which to the uninformed sounds
like a quotation from Mozart or Haydn and is in fact from the consequent to the lyrical theme in the Allegro moderato of Schubert's
E-flat major sonata for piano, op. 122, is the most inauthentic of all

in Mahler. The bell opening, so alien in a symphony, and the ostensibly naïve, dismantled, and reshuffled theme remain disparate. Nor is the instrumentation reassuring. The concertante solo wind intruments of the opening measures would be unthinkable in the Viennese classicism that the main theme evokes. With the logic of inconsistency more and more wind voices call the primacy of the strings into question; this happens in the continuation of the main theme, a consequent played by high horns that trace the melody with difficulty.[29] Entirely broken is the end of the song of heavenly joys, which Mahler no doubt had his reasons for excluding from the *Wunderhorn* cycle. These are not only the modest joys of the useful south German vegetable plot, full of toil and labor: "Sanct Martha die Köchin muss sein."[30] Immortalized in them are blood and violence; oxen are slaughtered, deer and hare run to the feast in full view on the roads. The poem culminates in an absurd Christology that serves the Savior as nourishment to famished souls and involuntarily indicts Christianity as a religion of mythical sacrifice: "Johannes das Lämmlein auslasset, der Metzger Herodes drauf passet" (John lets out the little lamb, for Herod the butcher to guard). Here the flutes intone the staccato eighth notes from the fool's introduction of the first movement and the clarinets its sixteenth-note figure. With the sad and risible intricacies of a rudimentary development the music unmistakably dims a paradise that it keeps pristine only when itself producing heavenly strains. The violin passage from the coda of the first movement, made famous by parodies, the three *sehr zurückhaltend* (very restrained) quarter notes before the last *grazioso* entry of the main theme,[31] are like a long backward look that asks: Is all that then true? To this music shakes its head, and must therefore buy courage with the caricaturing convention of the happy close of the pre-Beethovenian symphony and cancel itself out. Mahler's theology, again like Kafka's, is gnostic, his fairy-tale symphony as sad as the late works. If it dies away after the words of promise "that all shall awake to joy," no one knows whether it does not fall asleep forever. The phantasmagoria of the transcendent landscape is at once posited by it and negated. Joy remains unattainable, and no transcendence is left but that of yearning.

Even the Fourth, with its overflowing intentions, is not, however, program music. It differs from it not merely by using the so-called absolute forms sonata, scherzo, variations, song; the three last, extensive symphonic poems of Strauss also use these. Equally, even when he no longer had any truck with programs, Mahler cannot simply be subsumed under the practice of Bruckner or Brahms, or even the aesthetic of Hanslick. The composition has swallowed the program; the characters are its monuments. Mahler's real difference from the program is only fully discernible in the constellation of the characters with the banal. He does not subscribe to the program because he wishes neither to be exposed to the fortuitous appearance or otherwise of the poetic auxiliary ideas, nor to fix the meaning of the musical figures by decree. Characterization founders in Strauss because he defines the meanings purely from the standpoint of the subject, autonomously. This permits him his *trouvailles* down to *Elektra*, but at the same time hinders the compelling eloquence that to him meant everything. Instead, Mahler's medium is that of objective characterization. Each theme, over and above its mere arrangement of notes, has its distinct being, almost beyond invention. If the motives of program music await the labels of the textbooks and commentaries, Mahler's themes each bear their own names in themselves, without nomenclature. But such characterization has a prospect of validity only insofar as the musical imagination does not produce intentions at will, does not, therefore, think out motives that express this or that accordng to a plan, but works with a musical-linguistic material in which intentions are already objectively present. As preconceived entities they are quoted, as it were, by the musical imagination and dedicated to the whole. The materials that achieve this are those called banal, in which meaning has generally sedimented, before the advent of the individual composer, and has been punished by forfeiting the spontaneity of living execution. Such meanings stir anew under the staff of composition and feel their strength. They are reduced to elements of composition and at the same time freed from their thing-like rigidity. In this way Mahler's music is dedicated "concretely to the idea." Everywhere it is more than it would be merely by its parameters; but nowhere does it need, in order to understand in what way it is more, an abstract knowledge beyond its manifest form or the facile associations that might equally well be absent. To this extent the novelty of Mahler's conception is produced by what in isolation might be blamed as reactionary.

4

The reactionary element in Mahler's music is its naïveté. The inter-twinement of naïveté and sophistication in his work has always been a provocative contradiction: the physiognomy of a music that endows familiar popular phrases with meaning, while never doubting the self-evidence of its own high symphonic claims. Immediate and mediated elements are coupled because the symphonic form no longer guarantees musical meaning, both as a compelling set of relationships and as repository of truth, and because the form must seek that meaning. From a kind of basic musical existence, popular music, are to be derived the mediations by which alone existence is justified as meaningful. Thus, in historical-philosophical terms, Mahler's form approaches that of the novel. Pedestrian the musical material, sublime the execution. No different was the configuration of content and style in the novel of novels, Flaubert's *Madame Bovary*. Mahler's gesture is epic, and naïve: Listen, I am going to play something such as you have never heard. Like novels, each of his symphonies awakens the expectation of something special as a gift. Guido Adler's remark that no one, not even an opponent, has ever been bored by Mahler, relates to this. The early Mahler delighted in musical material that called for exuberance, in which there will have been no lack of Scheffelian fantasies. Underlying his spirituality was an element of the musical underworld. The fact that he sometimes demands "performance without any parody" and sometimes

"with parody," without the themes themselves giving any indica-
tion one way or the other, betrays the strained relation of his spirituality to high aspirations. It is not that music wants to narrate, but
that the composer wants to make music in the way that others narrate. By analogy with philosophical terminology this attitude would
be called nominalistic. The movement of the musical concepts begins from the bottom, as it were, with the facts of experience, trans-
mitting them in the unity of their succession and finally striking
from the whole the spark that leaps beyond the facts, instead of
composing from above, from an ontology of forms. To this extent
Mahler works decisively toward the abolition of tradition. At the
bottom of the musical novel form lies an aversion that must have
been felt long before Mahler, but that he was the first not to repress.
It is an aversion to knowing in advance how music continues. Knowing it offends musical intelligence, spiritual nervosity, Mahlerian
impatience. If after Mahler music cashed in its fixed elements, de-
valuing them to chips, he already protests against these from within
traditional musical logic. However, he does not construct new
forms, but sets neglected, despised, rejected ones in motion, those
that did not come under the official ontology of forms, which the
composing subject is neither able to fill on his own account, nor recognizes. Reified commodity characters interspersed in his music are
the necessary correlative of Mahler's nominalism, which no longer
permits any harmonious synthesis with a preconceived totality.
Symphonic objectivity can amalgamate with individual subjective
intentions only as discrete entities. Marches and *Ländler* in his work
correspond to the heritage of adventure stories and penny dreadfuls
in the bourgeois novel. Music's appeal against its split into an upper
and a lower sphere, which has left its mark on each, is pursued by
Mahler in such a way that the ferment induced in the lower sphere is
to restore by force what correctness in the upper has forfeited. By
this the strata of comprehensibility in Mahler are measured. He
might lay claim to the subtitle of *Zarathustra*, "Music for All and
None." Despite its conservative material, it is eminently modern in
offering no surrogate of a significant whole, staking everything on
alienated fortuitousness. If music up to Mahler really closed itself
anachronistically to the intellectual criticism of ideas and forms ex-

isting in themselves, behaving as if the Platonic starry sky arched above it, Mahler was the first to draw the musical conclusion from a state of consciousness that commands nothing but the hastily bundled profusion of its own impulses and experiences and the hope that something might arise from them which as yet they are not, but without falsification. That Mahler departs in principle from the Beethovenian type of intensive interlocking, the knot, renouncing dramaturgic concentration, is not sufficiently explained by the consideration that after Beethoven's *non plus ultra* on this ground no further advance was possible. The classicism of Beethoven's first movements—in the Eroica, the Fifth, and the Seventh—was no longer a model for Mahler because Beethoven's solution of recreating the subjectively weakened objective forms from further subjectivity could no longer be repeated with truthfulness. The difference of the epic ideal of composition from the classical type becomes the more visible the closer Mahler seems to approach it. The main theme of the Finale of the Fifth Symphony is orientated toward Beethoven in a way similar to that in Brahms's First, with a reverential allusion to the Hammerklavier sonata.[1] But this is only a pro forma main theme; it does not command the movement but is overgrown by others, is in a sense kept outside the door of the interior of the movement. For it announces precisely the older-style symphonic claim, the model to be analyzed and dramatically developed, to which the structure of Mahler's symphonic writing has become inappropriate in that it can no longer count on the emphatic self-confirmation of the internal architecture of music, the vehemence of which imbues the classical symphony. Even in Beethoven the static symmetry of the recapitulations threatened to disown the dynamic intent. The danger of academic form that increased after him is founded on the content. Beethovenian solemnity, the accentuation of meaning in the moment of symphonic release, reveals a decorative, illusory aspect. Beethoven's mightiest symphonic movements pronounce a celebratory "That is it" in repeating what has already existed in any case, present what is merely a regained identity as the Other, assert it as significant. The classical Beethoven glorifies what is because it cannot be other than it is by demonstrating its irresistibility.

The first movement of the Eroica, the Pastoral, the Ninth are ultimately only commentaries on what takes place in their opening measures. The mightiest intensifications that Beethoven has created—the lines from the beginnings of the Fifth and Seventh Symphonies to their conclusions—unroll with the overwhelming logic that the revelation of an ineluctably self-consistent event implies. It has the imperturbability of a mathematical formula and stands before us from the first moment to its last ramifications as an elemental fact. It is precisely in the irrefutable logical force of this art that its power resides, the unparalleled effect that Beethoven's symphonies have even today. It gave rise to the fundamental organic law that Beethoven could not escape even in the Ninth, the law that forcibly concentrated the basic idea in the opening phrase, the beginning, the theme, and evolved the whole organism as something ready-made from this beginning.[2]

What induced him, after the grandiosely retrospective first movement of the Ninth Symphony, to write the last quartets may not have been entirely different from the obscure instinct that motivated Mahler long before the years of his mastery: he was clearly profoundly impressed by the late Beethoven, above all by op. 135. Since Kant and Beethoven, German philosophy and music had been a single system. What it could not embrace, its corrective, took refuge in literature: the novel and a half-apocryphal tradition of the drama, until the category of life, etiolated as *Bildung* and usually reactionary, also became assimilable to philosophy around the turn of the century. In contrast, the originality of Mahler's music takes up Nietzsche's insight that the system and its seamless unity, its appearance of reconciliation, is dishonest. His music takes issue with extensive life, plunges with closed eyes into time, yet without installing life as a substitute metaphysics, in parallel to the objective tendency of the novel. His potential to do so derived from the partly prebourgeois feudal, partly Josephinistically skeptical Austrian air, untouched by German idealism, while symphonic integrity was still present enough to protect him from an attitude to form that made concessions to a weakly atomistic mode of listening.

He took from the theme as such its Beethovenian significance as a concentrating motto and gave it, through richer melodic elaboration, the character of an opening line that only gradually reveals its nature. This new kind of organic plan brought with it a new kind of thematic form. Beethoven's treatment of theme, that grandiose reflection of extreme compression of thought and unerring awareness of the goal, had no inner foundation in the new symphonic style which no longer knew of incessant striving from a creative spiritual centre but, on the contrary, had first to gather strength in the multiplicity of its appearances. Thus Beethoven's tight, thematically organic technique went out of use, or rather it became a subsidiary means.[3]

However, Bekker underestimates the extent to which Mahler mobilized the constructive forces of the system, however much he may have been perplexed by them. In the productive conflict of the contradictory elements his art flourishes. That is why it is so foolish to patronize him as a composer caught between ages.

His musical outlook was by no means lacking in tradition, a quasi-narrative, expansive undercurrent that in him strove toward the surface. Again and again in Beethoven the symphonic concentrates, which virtually supplant time, are matched by works whose duration is that of a joyous life both animated and reposing in itself. Among the symphonies the Pastoral represents this interest most ingenuously; the most important movements of the type include the first of the F major quartet, op. 59, no. 1. Toward the end of his so-called middle period it becomes more and more central to Beethoven's work, as in the first movements of the great B-flat major trio, op. 97, and the last violin sonata, pieces of supreme dignity. In Beethoven himself, confidence in extensive amplitude and in the possibility of passively discovering unity in multiplicity stylistically held in balance the tragic-classical idea of a music of the active subject. Schubert, for whom this idea had already paled, is all the more attracted by Beethoven's epic type. In the piano sonatas he sometimes casually disregards unity as Bruckner later did torpidly, in what was criticized as formlessness. Of all the precursors of Mahler's manner, the first movement of Schubert's B minor symphony must be the most important; it was revered by Webern as an entirely fresh conception of symphonic composition. Mahler was fascinated by the unfettered structure underlying the usual one; by the question where the individual themes, independently of their abstract status, seek to go; by the melancholy of a whole that does not presume to be in safety through being whole. From this aspect, moreover, it may be possible to unravel why Schubert's most magnificent conception remained a fragment, the first movement of music entirely organic and cleansed of rationalistic *vérités éternelles*. From it Mahler's aesthetic program is born. Among the Austrians before him the renunciation of a synthetic unity of apperception, a structural exertion of the subject, is punished by frequent flagging, a subsiding of the symphonic arch, and finally by a loss of organizing intellect itself, of technical legitimation. That is what Mahler seeks to correct in the tradition that is his own. The pronouncement attributed to him on Bruckner, his friend, "half god, half imbecile," is at least well coined; according to Bauer-Lechner he made plentiful critical comments on Bruckner, as on Schubert.[4] But what he censured in Bruckner was nothing other than the yawning gap between the emancipated, autonomous individual moments and the traditional architectonic norms. If Mahler's music—from the trio in the First, through the chorale of the Fifth and the close of the Seventh, to the conception of the Finale of the Ninth and the tone of the first movement of the Tenth—never conceals his gratitude to Bruckner, nevertheless his epic impulse seeks to master itself through construction, whereas in Schubert and Bruckner it often ebbs unreflectingly away. This lax element is coupled to activity, but not to strategic planning, rather a step-by-step advance as in a march. However preferable Bruckner's pristine underwood may seem to Mahler's brokenness, the latter surpasses a clumsiness in Bruckner, that obdurately static nuance that has no surer foundation than that Nietzsche was not yet much talked about in St. Florian. Mahler stood in relation to Bruckner as Kafka to Robert Walser. However, his corrective to the Austrian tradition was still Austrian: Mozart, in whom the unifying spirit and the uncurtailed freedom of details are reconciled. Hence, no doubt, the *hommage à Mozart* at the beginning of the Fourth. Asymmetry and irregularity of individual figures as of complexes and even of the form as a whole are not accidents of Mahler's nature, but necessitated by the epic intention. It is fond of the unanticipated, the unarranged, that which is subject to no compulsion, and, where compelled, it values divergence. Mahler's divergences are not substitutes as in Strauss, not surprising surrogates for the expected. Each irregularity stands specifically for itself. Even so, in what might well be called his musical empiricism, Mahler reflects on the meaning of the whole, which Bruckner's faith in authority took over from the symphonic form as such. He is mindful of what finds confirmation even in the most radical, disintegrated music: that transformed, disguised, and invisible objective forms, topoi, return where stubborn sensitivity avoids them. This return is facilitated by the ruins from which his architecture is piled up, much as Norman master builders in southern Italy may have made use of Doric columns. They obtrude as refractory outcrops, representatives of the element in the epic that cannot be reduced to mere subjectivity. What confronts the subject as concrete, hard, and even accidental must be assimilated by the composition into the experience of the immanent subject of the music. The musical situation from which Mahler speaks thereby becomes precarious. For neither is the musical language already so disqualified that the composing subject can manipulate it at will, freed of all preconceived forms and elements; nor are these elements so intact that they could in themselves organize the work. The delicacy of Mahler's music that was noticed from its first appearance results from this, not from the frailty of what Ernst Bloch a generation ago called his "mere talent."[5] The brokenness of Mahler's tone is the echo of that objective aporia, the schism of god and imbecile. Both, under the gaze of his music, become equally questionable, the god the immediate, dogmatic injunction to form, the imbecile the contingent, meaningless, potentially fatuous detail, capable of entering into no stringent relationship.

The concept of the epic explains certain eccentricities of Mahler that might otherwise easily be held against him. Despite all his critical vigilance against empty formality like that of Bruckner's sequences,

Mahler does not—as Beethoven does—shun lengthened measures, or moments in which, by the yardstick of musical action, nothing happens, but where the music becomes a state. Even in the highly controlled Ninth Symphony, immediately after the end of the exposition of the first movement, not only is there a full measure in which the timpani roll of the preceding final chord dies away, but the harmonic shift resulting from the addition of G-flat to the B-flat claims a further measure, still without motivic content, while the latter, the harp motive from the introduction, appears only in the third measure in the timpani. [6] A composer who feared delay would have made its introduction coincide with that of the G-flat. With artful nonchalance, in a field in the middle of the first movement of the Fourth Symphony, Mahler allows the movement to die, only to resume vigorously. [7] Instead of the outward flow being busily spurred on at the expense of the thematic figure's need of repose, Mahler relies on the inward flow; only the greatest composers can slacken the reins in this way without the whole slipping from their grasp. The works of Mahler the conductor are not infected by the gesture of the practical musician who in composing snaps his fingers, as it were, to make sure that everything goes without a hitch and no one's attention strays. In general, Mahler's music is never disfigured by the knowing experience of the interpreter. Nothing is composed out of consideration for the given empirical possibilities, never do the symphonies adapt themselves to practical demands. Without concessions they follow the imagination; practical experience is added in a secondary role, as a critical agency ensuring that what is imagined is also realized outwardly; in this Mahler is at the pole opposite the later kind of practical-mindedness embodied by Hindemith. Such tyrannical disregard for effects supports the epic intention; the agogic notation *Zeit lassen* (leave time) that occurs on occasion describes his manner as a whole. The constellation formed of patience with impatience is one of his peculiarities, a consciousness that neither denies time nor capitulates before it.

Mahler's epic-musical faith encounters a society in which music is no more able to "narrate" than to strike up a tune. Mahler escapes the abominable aura of the word *Musikant*—"minstrel"—in that his underlying forms are modeled on the novel rather than on the epic, despite a courage to linger without the trappings of majestic rootedness. He holds the attention first by always proceeding differently than expected, and so is gripping in the exact sense. Erwin Stein, in a forgotten essay in *Pult und Taktstock,* remarked on this decades ago. Mahler's impassioned relation to Dostoevsky[8] is known, a writer who stood in 1890 for something other than in the age of Möller van den Bruck. On an excursion with Schoenberg and his followers, Mahler is said to have advised him to study less counterpoint and read more Dostoevsky, only to hear Webern's heroically timid riposte: "Pardon, *Herr Direktor,* but we have Strindberg." This probably apocryphal anecdote illuminates the difference between the novelistic musical disposition and the Expressionist one of the next, fully emancipated generation of composers. But it is not only that Mahler's music so often sounds as if it were trying to tell something that calls to mind the great novel. The curve it describes is novelistic, rising to great situations, collapsing into itself.[9] Gestures are enacted like that of Natasha in *The Idiot,* throwing bank notes into the fire; or like the one in Balzac, when the criminal Jacques Collin, disguised as a Spanish canon, restrains the young Lucien de Rubempré from suicide and assists him to a period of splendor; perhaps also that of Esther, who sacrifices herself for her lover without suspecting that in the meantime the roulette of life has rescued both from all their wretchedness. As in novels, happiness flourishes in Mahler on the brink of catastrophe. Everywhere in his work images from novels are at work latently or openly as centers of force. Happiness is for him the figure of meaning in prosaic life, the utopian fulfillment of which is vouched for by the unhoped for and invisible winnings of the gambler. In Mahler happiness remains as much chained to its opposite as that of the gambler to loss and ruin. Luxuriating and squandering themselves without reason or self-preserving control, the elevations in the Finale of the Sixth Symphony bear their downfall teleologically within themselves. In tireless overexertion, brooking no resignation, Mahler's music traces an electrocardiogram, the history of the breaking heart. Where it overtaxes itself, it expresses the possibility of the world that the world refuses, for which there are no words in the world's language; this truest of all things is discredited as the world's untruthfulness.

As in the great novels—and perhaps musically only previously in the second act of *Die Walküre*—the ephemeral fulfillment is to outweigh all else: he believes in no form of eternity except the transient one. Like the philosophy of Hegelian phenomenology, music in Mahler is the objective life all over again, now penetrating the subject, and its re-emergence in the inner world transfigures it into a stirring absolute. In the same way the concrete act of reading a novel exists in a dimension different from the distinct perception of events. The ear is carried along on the flow of the music as is the eye of the reader from page to page; the mute sound of the words converges with the musical mystery. But the mystery is not solved. To describe the world to which epic music alludes is denied to it: the music is as clear as it is cryptic. It can make the ontological categories of objective reality its own only insofar as it screens itself from objective immediacy; it would remove itself from the world if it tried to symbolize or even depict it. Schopenhauer and Romantic aesthetics discovered this when they reflected on the shadowy and dreamlike quality of music. But music does not so much paint shadowy and dreamlike states of the soul as, in terms of logic and appearance, it is itself related to the soul of dream and shadow. It takes on being, as a reality sui generis, through derealization. This shadowy medium, that of all music, becomes thematic to an extent in Mahler. Twice he uses the word *schattenhaft* (shadowy) as an expression mark, in the Scherzo of the Seventh Symphony and in the first movement of the Ninth.[10] The metaphor from the optical realm indicates externality as a complement to music's inner space. To the extent that everything musical, intensified to a sensuous certainty, occupies that inner space, nothing is disdained and excluded as mere material. In the musical space an empirical realm of the second degree flourishes, one that is no longer, like the other, heteronomous to the art-work. The inwardness of music assimilates the outward, instead of representing, externalizing, the inward. So much is true in the psychoanalytical theory that interprets music as a defense against paranoia: it protects the subject from an overwhelming reality by subjective projection. It does not confuse the world, which it names as its equal, with itself, nor are its categories the disconnected ones of the mere subject: they remain directed at those of the world.

If the latter were directly equated to being—and as understood by Schopenhauer it is music that is immediate being—music would be madness. All great music is snatched from madness; all music harbors the identification of inward and outward, but over the outcome madness has no power. Music sanctions the separation of being and object as its own boundary to the objective; thus it appropriates being. That Mahler, who spent his life in the opera and whose symphonic impulse runs parallel to that of opera in so many ways, wrote no operas may be explained by the transfiguration of the objective into the inner world of images. His symphony is *opera assoluta*. Like the opera, Mahler's novelistic symphonies rise up from passion and flow back into it; passages of fulfillment such as are found in his works are better known to opera and the novel than to otherwise absolute music.

Mahler's relation to the novel as a form can be demonstrated, for example, by his inclination to introduce new themes, or at least to disguise thematic material so that in the course of the movements it appears quite new. After preliminary appearances in the first movements of the First and Fourth, this tendency becomes pronounced in the second movement of the Fifth where, after one of the slow interpolations, a somewhat secondary figure from the exposition[11] is taken up and reformulated,[12] as if, unexpectedly, a previously unregarded person now entered the scene to assist development, as in Balzac and, in the earlier Romantic novel, in Walter Scott; Proust is said to have pointed out that in music new themes sometimes take over the center in the same way as previously unnoticed minor characters in novels. The formal category of the new theme derives paradoxically from the most dramatic of all symphonies. But precisely the singular case of the Eroica throws Mahler's formal intention into relief. In Beethoven the new theme comes to the aid of a deliberately overextended development, as if the latter could no longer clearly recall the distant exposition. Nevertheless, the new theme does not really cause surprise, but enters as something prepared, something familiar; not by chance have analysts repeatedly attempted to derive it from the material of the exposition. The classical idea of the symphony takes for granted a definite, closed multiplicity just as Aristotelian poetics assumes the three unities. A theme appearing as absolutely new offends its economic principle, that of reducing all events to a minimum of postulates, an axiom of completeness that integral music has made as much its own as have systems of knowledge since Descartes's *Discours de la méthode*. Unforeseen thematic components destroy the fiction that music is a pure tissue of deductions, in which everything that happens follows with unambiguous necessity. In this, too, Schoenberg and his school were truer to the classical ideal of the "obligatory," which is now showing its questionable elements, than was Mahler. In the latter, even figures that, as in the Fifth, were indeed motivically developed from what had gone before, become fresh entities removed from the machinery of the process. Where the dramatic symphony believes it takes hold of its idea with an inexorable rigor derived from the model of discursive logic, the novel-symphony seeks to escape that logic: it craves the open air. And in general Mahler's themes are recognizable, like characters in a novel, as developing themes that retain their essence unchanged. In this, too, he departs from the classical ideal of music, in which the precedence of the whole over the parts is the uncontested priority of becoming over being, in which the whole itself virtually produces the themes and penetrates them dialectically. In Mahler, conversely, the thematic figure is no more indifferent to the symphonic flow than are the characters in a novel to the dimension of time within which they act. Driven on by impulses, as the same beings they yet become different, shrink, expand, even age. This modification of fixed elements, which becomes ingrained in the novel, is as unclassical as the toleration of an individual musical identity, the inextinguishable character of thematic figures. As soon as traditional great music ceased "working out" through a development, it was content with a conserved architectonic identity; if an element recurred identically it was, aside from the key, identical and nothing else. Mahler's symphonic writing, however, sabotages these alternatives. Nothing in them is ever entirely consumed by the dynamic, but nothing ever remains what it was. Time passes into the characters and changes them as empirical time alters faces.

The dramatic-classical symphony beguiles time by converting it into spirit, as if moved by a feudal desire to avoid tedious protraction, to kill time made inward as an aesthetic law. But the epic type of symphony enjoys time to the full, abandons itself to it, seeks to make physically measurable time into living duration. Duration in it is itself the imago of meaning—perhaps to resist the encroaching anullment of duration in the production method of late industrialism and the forms of consciousness adapted to it. No longer is time to be subjected to a musical *trompe-l'oreille*; it is not to masquerade as the moment it is not. The antithesis of this was already Schubert's "heavenly length." Not only are the melodies, from which his instrumental movements are sometimes unwilling to tear themselves away, so complete in themselves that the thought of development applied to them is unseemly; but also the desire to fill up time with music, to resist transience by that which has the right to abide, itself becomes a musical wishful image. It too has its prehistory; it was difficult enough in Bach's time to wrest temporal extension for music. To lament over Mahlerian *longueurs* is no more reputable than the attitude that sells abridged versions of Fielding or Balzac or Dostoevsky. To be sure, the prodigal extension of time in Mahler makes hardly less stringent demands on ears trained to discern commodities than had symphonic compression earlier; where the latter required the sharpest concentration, the former demands the unconditional readiness of patience. Mahler makes no concessions to the comfort of "easy listening" without remembrance or expectation. The composition elaborates duration. If Beethoven's contemporaries quailed before the accelerated time of his symphonies as before the first railroads with their allegedly detrimental effects on the nerves, those who have survived Mahler by fifty years flinch at his works as the habitués of air travel shrink from a voyage by sea. Mahlerian duration reminds them that they have themselves lost duration; perhaps they fear that they no longer live at all. They fend this off with the important man's superior assertion that he has no time, which lets slip its own ignominious truth. It is absurd to make Mahler and Bruckner palatable by deletions, which, in Otto Klemperer's bon mot, make their movements longer, not shorter. Nothing in them is dispensable; where something is missing the whole becomes chaos. Almost a hundred years after Schubert mere length is, for Mahler's music, no longer divine. Patiently as it flows out into time, just as impatiently it watches to ensure that this time is filled with musical content; the critical question is the active principle of its form. Through relentless elaboration of the details and their relations it gives notice to conformism, both the conformism of Austrian coziness and that of all musical culture that has degenerated to consumption. In their duration his *moments musicaux* weigh no less heavily than those of Schubert, to whom the expression dates back. For it is only when mediated through their intensity, and not as a crammed span, that extensive time in them becomes a plenitude.

The link between the novelesque nature and the ductus of Mahler's music are the songs. Their function in relation to his symphonic writing cannot be subsumed, on the pattern of Wagner's *Wesendonk-Lieder*, under the facile concept of preparatory studies. Through their own symphonic element they are distinct from almost every other musical lyric of the same period; a precondition of this is the archaic choice of texts, which holds studiously aloof from the psychologically individualized ego. Richard Specht has contributed an ineffable introduction to the pocket edition of the scores of Mahler's orchestral songs. He does not shrink from asserting: "Such may have been the songs of soldiers, shepherds, and country folk in the small market towns of earlier centuries,"[13] undeterred in such fatuity by the "unique instrumentation": "here is a delicacy, a variety of nuances of color that has become attainable only in our time, the time after Wagner and Berlioz,"[14] whereas their art not only precludes performance at fairs and markets, which in any case no longer exist, but contradicts the very concept of the folk song. However, in the midst of such contaminations, Specht surprises the reader with the observation that in Mahler we are not concerned with the subjective lyric. Paul Bekker has made this insight fruitful:

> In Mahler the song converges with an urge toward monumentality. The song is raised from the confining expression of subjective feelings to the radiant and sonorous sphere of symphonic style. This in turn enriches its expansive force with the intimacy of personal feeling. This appears paradoxical, and yet

it is just such a union of opposites that explains the strange nature of Gustav Mahler's work, which encompasses both the inner and outer worlds, embracing both the most personal and the most remote in its expressive range. It explains the outward contradictions of his work, which often seems to mingle indiscriminately the most disparate stylistic elements. It explains the divergent evaluations of his music. [15]

Not till *Das Lied von der Erde,* which styles itself a symphony, does Mahler, not without difficulty, espouse the idea of the subjective lyric. In that respect he is an outsider in the history of the German song from Schubert to Schoenberg and Webern, and in line rather with Mussorgsky, in whom such objectivity has been noted on occasion, or with Janáček; perhaps Hugo Wolf, in passages that transcend the normal limits of a text to be set to music, was groping for something similar; in precisely this moment Mahler may have had an essential point of contact with the Slavic East, as a prebourgeois, not yet entirely individualized milieu. Mahler puts these songs into the mouth of someone other than the music's subject. They do not sing of themselves, but narrate, being epic lyrics like the children's songs from whose practice at least Mahler's earlier songs derive in their broken recurrence of melodies of dance and play. Their flow is a kind of storytelling, and their expression a commentary on the story. Such stylized objectivity forms the homogeneous medium of Mahler's songs and symphonies. The former unfold in the symphonies as they would in principle have liked to do within themselves. The totality of the symphonies is that of the world of which the songs sing. The irrational tendency of the *Wunderhorn* poems toward the absurd, resulting from the montage of divergent poems, as noted by Goethe in his review, [16] is vindicated by Mahler's mode of composition: it invites that musical coherence that owes as little to concepts as to psychology. The folk and musically subjective elements interact in such a way that the residue of the absurd, the refuge of music in the text, is organized, "rationalized" by music according to its own laws. But as Mahler's song compositions stand in relation to the poems, his symphonies proceed as a whole with regard to their thematic nuclei. The unifying element of lyric and symphony is the ballade, and Mahler was no doubt being indiscreet when, in a purely instrumental movement, at a moment of breathless tension, he quoted an earlier instrumental piece bearing the title *Ballade*, Chopin's G minor Ballade, in the second movement of the Fifth Symphony.[17] As strophic songs Mahler's songs have a balladesque objectivity, while the subjective lyric sacrifices the strophic structure to that of the poem and the musical form. Hence the especial difficulty of performing Mahler's orchestral songs. They realize the strophic character yet modify the stanzas as the narrative advances. What they narrate is the musical content itself; they recite themselves. That music recites itself, is its own content, narrates without narrative, is no tautology, nor a metaphor for the habitus of the narrator, which unquestionably fits much in Mahler. The relation of diction to discourse in music of his kind is that between the particular elements and the general flow. The discourse is made up of the concrete individual figures, the musical "content" in the narrower sense. The diction, however, is the flow of the whole. In that the individual elements are carried by it, in a sense it depicts them; the reflection of the details by the context is of the same nature as the reflection of a narrated incident by the narrative. Vulgar as the distinction between form and content is in face of a work of art, just as feeble is the abstract assertion of their identity; only when both elements are held apart are they identifiable as one and the same. As mediated elements they are preserved in their distinctness, and just this is achieved by the epic gesture of a music that relates itself. In it the riddle of all art takes on, in Mahler, a form that torments the onlooker, the more insistently the better he understands it, with the question as to what art is and ought to accomplish. Like the storyteller, Mahler's music never says the same thing twice in the same way: in this way subjectivity plays a part. Through it the unforeseeable, the contingent matter that it tells becomes, as form, a surprise, the principle of ever-changingness, by which alone time, as an emphatic reality, is really constituted. Accordingly, Mahler's songs should never be performed in conveyerbelt fashion without temporal articulation—"Rewelge," with its marking *In einem fort* (continuously), being the one exception that proves the rule, for the sake of a march that even death does not in-

terrupt. The artificial objectivity of Mahler's songs, the archetype
of that of his symphonies, ought to clarify why they all, after the
first three collections, are given an orchestral accompaniment.
Mahler resisted the piano as the clattering, reified instrument of
subjective lyrics that it had become in his time, while the orchestra
permitted a twofold effect: to register the musical idea precisely in
concrete color, and to establish, through the choric volume that it
retains even in pianissimo, a kind of inner largeness. The mere
sound elicits a We as the musical subject, whereas the accompanied
song of the nineteenth century had installed itself in the home of the
individual bourgeois person. As ballades Mahler's songs organize
themselves according to the formal law of the narrative, a time continuum of successive, essentially related yet distinct events. The
strophic, but never mechanically repetitive, time-abolishing super-
imposition of musical fields is carried over to symphonic writing.
While its objectivity is supported by the old compulsion to repeat, it
also breaks it by the perpetual production of the new. From the time-
lessness of the unchanging Mahler releases historical time. He
thereby takes up the anti-mythological tendency proper originally
to the epic and later, especially, to the novel.[18] The proximity is
most unconcealed in some of Mahler's first movements, which are
least hindered by the static quality of dance-like schemata. They
have to rid themselves of the recapitulation. Either they so abbrevi-
ate it that in face of the preponderance of development it hardly
counts, or they radically modify it. In the first movement of the
Third Symphony the sonata pattern is really no more than a husk
over the intrinsic, unfettered course of the form. In it Mahler takes
greater risks than he ever did again, its complicity with chaos sur-
passing even that of the Finale of the First. No less monstrous than
the disproportions in the movement is its length. The panic abundance, which virtually erases the controlling musical subject, ex-
poses itself to every critical objection. As is not uncommon for
innovative composers, Mahler appears to have taken fright; the
next work was the highly stylized, tautened Fourth. Striking in the
first movement of the Third is the waiving of all the well-tried
categories of mediation. In a way similar to that of the expressionist
Schoenberg, the complexes are not artfully woven together. Exul-

tantly barbarous, Mahler connects them with the mere rhythm of
the percussion, an abstract rapping of time. The smoothing, harmo-
nizing process of mediation is disdained; Mahler offers up chunks,
not broth. Even within the introduction an "empty" connecting
space is audaciously created beyond the musical movement.[19] It is
not merely by academic rules that, later, the transition to the recapitulation by side drums alone appears absurd.[20] But in face of the
genius of this passage such objections reel helplessly, like the aesthetics of the *juste milieu*. The development is swept aside, as if the
composing subject were tired of intervening in his music and left it
to come unmolested to self-awareness. Themes in the normal sense
are lacking, as they were already in the first movement of the Second, where one main theme was replaced by a recitative of the basses
and its *cantus firmus*-like counterpoint. But in the first movement
of the Third the complexes of which it is composed no longer exist
tectonically at all, but come into being before the listener's ears, especially blatantly where the recapitulation of the march does not
simply begin, but seems to become gradually audible again, as if latently it had always continued playing.[21] The opening theme, which
might initially be confused with a first theme, is, as Bekker has observed, rather an abbreviation than material for elaboration. Its
characteristic intervals of descending seconds, however, are those of
one of the march motives, which will be most important later.[22] The
proportions of the movement are primeval. The improvisatory introduction, built up of two gigantic parallel sections, overshadows
the exposition and recapitulation of the march, which would have
corresponded to sonata form; it is balanced, however, by the equally
immoderate development. The literary idea of the great god Pan has
invaded the sense of form; form itself becomes something both
fearful and monstrous, the objectification of chaos; nothing else is
the truth of the concept of nature, especially misused in relation to
this movement. Rhythmically irregular woodwind fragments continually interject voices of nature; the combination of march and
improvisation touches on the principle of chance. Nowhere does
Mahler less rigorously censor the banal; now there are snatches of
"Ich hab mich ergeben mit Herz und mit Hand" (surrendered have I
with heart and with hand), now of Mendelssohn's *Midsummer*

Night's Dream overture, while the patriotic song about the Field Marshal from school songbooks cuts in shrilly as if it had never referred to the old Blücher. The movement cranes and stretches itself in all directions like a gigantic body. It has no time for polyphony. The principal material of the development, the B-flat minor entry,[23] although it is maintained solo for a few measures as if about to lead into a fugue, then attaches itself in a most un-fuguelike manner to a single note, and anyone expecting the well-bred answer has been duped. Older idiomatic elements like the Schubertian ornamental turns, are potentiated to surprise attacks on civilization. The last movement of the Sixth inherited from this one the question of the possibility of a kind of musical novel in several volumes and responded with inexorable construction. The Third, however, thumbs its nose at the thought of order and yet is so crammed with material and so rigorously composed that it never slackens. This organization of the disorganized it owes to a singular awareness of time. If its first movement achieves a true sonata exposition, this is not simply, as the rhythm suggests, a long march; rather, the second proceeds as if the musical subject were marching with a band playing all kinds of marches one after another. The formal impulse is the idea of a spatially moving source of music.[24] Like much recent music, the movement, in its inner structure, has a shifting, not a fixed, frame of reference. Yet the result is not an impressionistic, timelessly spatialized interpenetration of sounds as in Debussy's *Feux d'artifice* with the July 14 fanfare; instead, the juxtaposed fragments of marches create, through their exact proportions, articulated history. At one point it comes to resemble a breakthrough;[25] a march *Abgesang* follows[26] until—but without any sense of catastrophe, rather as if a new aspect were suddenly revealed—the whole of the march music collapses.[27] The excessively enlarged development then brings the anti-architectonic character of the exposition back within the architecture. Its structure corresponds in its roughest outlines, as is not uncommon in Mahler and occasionally occurred in Viennese classicism, to what has happened up to the development, naturally without crude parallels. It could be analyzed as a kind of first varied recapitulation carried to the extreme, followed by a second, the recapitulation in the narrower sense. Through the hint of a repetition the exposition retrospectively becomes an architectonic wing of the piece, while the utterly loose treatment of the development, which never moves purposefully toward a goal and finally loses itself,[28] stays true to the anti-architectonic intention. The first section of the development at first resembles a recapitulation, as equivalent to the exposition of the introduction.[29] It leads through a wan answering phrase on the English horn[30] into the next section. This is an analogue of the vague foreground of the original march; the pallor of the introduction is transmitted to it.[31] The third part uses march components but, in consequence of the weaker lighting, with a lyrical tone, a clearly interpolated episode in G-flat.[32] The fourth section of the development, finally, like some of the closing, decisive parts of Beethoven's developments, opens with abrupt resolve,[33] wrenching itself as violently from the tendency of the movement as the latter had earlier overwhelmed the forces of control.

5

How the individual element, emancipated in novel-like fashion from fixed schemata, takes on form and inaugurates autonomous connections within itself becomes a specific problem of Mahler's technique. It has to elaborate the Mahlerian parodoxicalness, a totality without an outline, a synthesis of the open and the closed. This is already hinted at in a famous but naïve dictum of the young Mahler, that writing a symphony is "constructing a world with all the technical means at one's disposal."[1] Here technique appears as something extraneous to the music, to be used in the service of the intention. The title "Symphony of a Thousand," which concert managements attached, to his disgust, to the Eighth Symphony in 1910, exploits this aspect. Music that seeks to reduplicate the world wishes to make use of everything the world offers, without troubling overmuch how far what is available in compatible with its idea. However, Mahler's notion of technique is rapidly driven by its own logic beyond that initial standpoint. As the mere resource of the orchestral means and the other ostensible acquisitions of the time, technique would be no less external to the music than was the traditional canon of forms. Because the composer's comfort assorts ill with Mahler's uncomfortable intentions, he does not master that kind of technique as effortlessly as Strauss, the model music student as genius. He must laboriously acquire, for example by the belated study of Bach, what composers as steeped in their culture as Debussy have from the start. The existing means do not suit Mahler's intention, which is aimed at the non-existent. He must not only learn them, but avoid much that they contain, like Wagner's opulent sound or the élan, coursing unabashed toward wholeness, of a Strauss genial even in his excesses. He projects a changed idea of technique itself, an integral technique relating to the essence of musical coherence. In it all musical dimensions are involved as partial elements; he leaves none of them unchallenged. From resistance to the mastery of others that had degenerated to facility, from the unpolished and provocative awkwardness of the First and Third Symphonies, a mastery is reinstated that finally, through the identity of the composed and its appearance, leaves the technical standard of the time beneath it; with Mahler in mind, Alban Berg objected in Strauss precisely to his technique. That each of Mahler's works criticizes its predecessor makes him the developing composer par excellence; if anyone, it is in Mahler's far from copious oeuvre that one can speak of progress. What he improves always becomes something different; hence the highly un-Brucknerian medley of his successive symphonies. The rehearsal technique of a conductor who was fond of retouching and revising instrumentation may have schooled the composer in permanent self-correction. Even where he goes back to earlier work of his own, there is progress. In the first *Nachtmusik* of the Seventh Symphony the *Wunderhorn* songs shed a fluorescent glow of something already irrecoverable. Long stretches of the Eighth, in which analogies to the Second have been noted, sound straightforwardly diatonic after the bolder harmony of the Seventh. Strauss is said, after its Munich première, to have poked fun at the amount of E-flat major. But like a seed leaf it covers surprisingly much from the late phase, even including reminiscences of "Von der Jugend" from *Das Lied von der Erde*. Mahler's hard developmental line, like that of major exponents of the New Music, writes musical history as the composer progresses from work to work. Schoenberg behaved just as energetically, whereas in Strauss the movement is arrested with suicidal caution after *Elektra*, and in Reger, once the panchromatic procedure has been established, hardly any movement takes place. Not they, but Mahler alone was accorded a late style of that supreme rank that, in Alban Berg's maxim, decides the dignity of a composer. It had already not escaped

Bekker's notice that the last works of one who hardly passed the age of fifty are late works in the most emphatic sense: they turn ascetic inwardness outwards. But how much Mahler's critical will contributed to his development can be shown already in his middle period. In the Seventh Symphony he neither forgets what he achieved in the Sixth nor does he merely rehash it. Imagination focuses a beam of light on its contours, in which they are unrecognizable. The conductor's productive irritability may have been irked by some ossifying details in the Sixth, above all the Scherzo; he was never entirely satisfied with the original published version and revised the instrumentation extensively; his last arrangement of the movements, with the E-flat major Andante before the Finale, should be respected, if only for the modulation scheme; E-flat major is the relative of C minor, with which the Finale begins, only to decide, after long preparation, on A minor as its principal key. Mahler found an antidote to rigidity in the élan of Richard Strauss, which is perceptible in the first movement of the Seventh, directly before the recapitulation of the introduction and then, above all, before that of the first theme.[2] The first conspicuous stage in Mahler's development was the Fourth Symphony, which probably for that reason so drastically curtailed the "available technical means." The qualitative leap after it, despite the subterranean passages linking the Fourth and the Fifth, is undisputed. It is hardly the case, as a nugatory interpretation has it, that the middle works stand foursquare on solid ground, in contrast to the allegedly metaphysical earlier ones. Nevertheless, their texture is incomparably richer, and also tauter; they really know the world better. What was projected earlier is to be executed now; the elements of the *Wunderhorn* symphonies are reflected—for example, the trumpet fanfare from the first movement of the Third in the introduction to the Finale of the Sixth.[3] A Mahler far detached from himself imposes authenticity on his precocious earlier formulations; for this reason the middle symphonies, essentially productive repetitions, tolerate routine elements, in places where their self-control is not exercised intrusively, in a way that is not encountered in the spontaneous outpouring of the youthful works. Only in the late phase does Mahler retrospectively attain a second immediacy. His musical intelligence is objectified through self-reflection, like those of Beethoven and Brahms before him, not as a subjective property of the composer but as an attribute of the music itself, which grows aware of itself and so becomes the Other. The achievements of Mahler's technique are its own, a concern for plastic composition and thus for graphic representation. This led the composer, swiftly labeled romantic by musical history, out of the sway of Romanticism. Similar to Wagner's his work dreams of a manner of composing that is disenchanted, lacks brilliance, does not transfigure. Through it, the work schooled itself in the firm negation of the musical ideology of the period. Mahler reacted violently against musical stupidity, which spread itself no less in the nineteenth century than in the eighteenth and seventeenth; he was nauseated by infantile repetition. But he was also aware that the tectonic element, primitively represented by repetition, cannot be extirpated. With this contradiction his intelligence has to come to terms. Everything that made up the allure of the symphonies of his youth, particularly the Second, becomes indifferent in face of this.

The Mahlerian technique that advanced in this way had its *differentia specifica* from that of other composers in the variant, as opposed to the variation. Mahler too, in the Adagio of the Fourth, wrote variations; other places, such as the Finale of the Ninth, at least resemble variations. But the principle of variation does not define, as with Schoenberg, the make-up of his music, its *peinture*. The Mahler variant is the technical formula for the epic and novel-like element of the always different yet identical figures. Any set of variations by Beethoven could be compared with any song by Mahler, such as "Der Schildwache Nachtlied." In Beethoven some individual structural elements, primarily the use of a melodic bass line, are kept the same; others, like the figuration or the placement of the main constituent motives, are systematically modified from variation to variation. In Mahler, after the first interpolation of the girl's stanza, the opening theme is repeated unquestioned, except for conspicuous individual modifications like the replacement of the dominant of B-flat major in the first measure by the dominant of the relative key G minor, then of the submediant of B-flat major by an ambiguous augmented triad and, further, of the transitional measure on the tonic of B-flat major by the tonic of G minor, but with a faithfully matching continuation until the next difference three measures later. Everywhere the overall structure is unmistakably preserved, but everywhere punctuated with artifices, the inversion of harmonic proportions like those of major and minor sonorities as compared with their first appearance and, thereby, the revocation of the opening formulation of the theme, as if it were subject to the whims of improvisation. The general outlines of Mahler's themes always remain intact. They are gestalten, as the term is used in psychological theory for the primacy of the whole over the parts. Within this explicit yet vague identity, however, the concrete musical content, above all the sequence of the intervals, is not fixed. If in Beethoven's thematic process it is precisely the smallest motivic cells of the themes that determine their elaboration into qualitatively different theme complexes; if in that composer the thematic macrostructure is a technical result, in Mahler by contrast the musical microorganisms are incessantly modified within the unmistakable outlines of the main figures, most relentlessly in the first movement of the Third Symphony. The nature of Mahler's themes qualifies them to work better on the level of themes than of motives. Their smallest elements are blurred to the point of irrelevance, because the wholes themselves do not sufficiently represent fixed values to be split up into differentials. Instead, more extensive groups are recalled with that vagueness often enough displayed by musical memory. This makes it possible to revise their nuances, their lighting, and finally their characters, so that the variants impinge after all on the large themes and finally take on tectonic functions, without the themes needing to be dissected in terms of motives. Such largesse in the treatment of his material, again contrary to the principle of economy of Beethoven and Brahms, legitimizes technically the large scale of Mahler's epic symphonic writing. He thinks in terms of complexes, fields. He has nothing of that form of musical reaction that desires contraction at all costs and which, after him, at times claimed exclusivity. The sweep of his symphonic movement derives not from the pent-up, onward-driving force of Beethoven, but from the amplitude of a hearing encompassing the far distance, to which the most remote analogies and consequences are virtually present as to the narrative that is master of itself.

In Mahler's conception of the theme as a gestalt with mobile motivic content the practice of Schoenberg's twelve-tone technique is prefigured, with its tendency toward stable rhythmic patterns filled with tones in changing row forms. Because Mahler's themes, being relatively stable, are not altered in a continuous development, they are not initially expounded either. The concept of the theme as a given, then to be modified, is inadequate to Mahler. Rather, the nucleus undergoes a treatment similar to that of a narrative element in oral tradition; at each telling it becomes slightly different. The principle of the variant arises in the strophic song with variations, insofar as its stanzas too cannot be radically varied. Antipsychological in the manner of ballades, like refrains they recur as formulas and yet are as free of rigidity as Homeric formulas. What has happened and will happen affects them. Nor do they remain isolated, but often intermingle. The most usual deviations occur at the critical joins, descendents of the ends of stanzas. The relations between these deviations, the degree of proximity or distance between them, their proportions and syntactic connections, make up the concrete logic, which cannot be boiled down to a general rule, of Mahler's epic manner of composing. But if the technique of variant stimulates the formal process in a work, at the same time the variant is itself a prototype of this form, as something unchanging like musical language and yet evolving through its deviation from this language. The firm, identical core, which nevertheless exists, is difficult to pin down, as if it shunned mensural notation. No theme is positively, unambiguously there, none is ever quite definitive; they submerge in and re-emerge from the time continuum, which is itself constituted equally by their indefinite nature and the rigor of their deviations. To this extent the variants are the countervailing force to fulfillment. They divest the theme of its identity; the fulfillment is the positive manifestation of what the theme has not yet become. In some movements that make use of main themes in a normal configuration, they protrude strangely from the actual musical process, as if it were not their own history; Paul Bekker already attested that the theme of the Andante in the Sixth Symphony, a theme with an entirely closed structure, seems to strive to be forgotten during the piece. If one comes upon something inertly reified, derivative, in Mahler's thematic nuclei, this non-spontaneous element for its part mocks the reifications of the theory of form. In that they are not freely posited by the subject and assert their inauthenticity against its presumption of control, they also escape the hand of the composer who was chiseling them to their definitive shape. They have no walls within the form, and their relationships create that perspective of a whole that is normally suppressed by the song-like rounded themes of post-Beethoven Romanticism. Themes that are preserved but not firmly congealed and that seem to emerge from a collective world of images are reminiscent of Stravinsky. But Mahler's variants are not irregular, lopsidedly arranged, unrelated cubes. They do not bring time to a standstill, but are produced by it and produce it as a consequence of the fact that one cannot step twice into the same river. Mahlerian duration is dynamic. The extreme otherness of his continuations does not wear a mask of mimed unchangingness, but clings tightly to the contour of time by scenting something reified even in the traditional kind of subjective dynamic, the rigid contrast between that which is once given, and what it becomes. His principle is not violence but its negation. The advancing movement accommodates the qualitative implications of the figures. Mahler's technique of the variant penetrates as far as the musical idiom that animates these figures. The variants are the theater of his dialect; the standard language is glimpsed through them, but the words sound nearer, different. The variants are always technical formulas of deviation from that which is in the right, which writes history, the official version that has come out on top. It is as a differentness of the familiar that the variant probably first exerted its attraction on Mahler. In the shrill E-flat clarinet passage in the Second Symphony marked *mit Humor* (with humour),[4] it would still be possible to make out how the section would have sounded undistorted. Later Mahler's variants are no longer conveniently legible as caricatures of the orthodox, but are determined by the composition itself. For this the musical language offers starting

points that Mahler inherited; inflections of the Austrian musical
tradition are steeped in deviations, such as those of Schubert compared with Mozart.

The variant technique may be rooted in an experience that
every musical person is likely to have had early on and that is only
overgrown by a respect to which Mahler was immune through his
respect for the matter itself: that variations frequently prove a dis-
appointment after their theme, that they hold on to it, depriving it
of its nature without truly developing it into something different.
Thus the theme is almost always disfigured in older figural variations, but also in those of the Beethovenian type, like some in the
second movement of the Kreutzer Sonata. The Mahlerian variant
subjects them to productive criticism. By its law the deviation may
never weaken the intensity or meaning of the model. Sometimes, in
Mahler, motives take over the role of the joker in a pack of cards, the
ornamentally transposed images of which bear a general resemblance to Mahler's music; it sometimes has the air of playing-
card kings. One is liable to gloss over the variants of such joker motives as if they happened by chance; an element of the fortuitous in
their changes is no less inherent in their meaning than chance is in
games of hazard. But the gaze that lingers discovers a musical logic
even in them. One of them is formed additively from the ending of
the first and the beginning of the second half of a phrase of the main
theme in the opening movement of the Fourth Symphony,[5] the
kingdom of the bell. It is accompanied by the subdominant. Its closing segment is immediately amputated,[6] and a first variant follows
directly.[7] It still touches the subdominant in the accent part of the
measure, but leaves it in the second with a deviaton into A minor,
the composed-out supertonic degree of the main tonality. The harmony is intensified as compared to the elementary form of its first
appearance, whereas the melody weakens. With an identical
rhythm, the characteristic rising second in the first half is inverted,
and in the sixteenth notes the F-sharp climax is avoided: it remains,
with a tone repetition, on E. But this decrescendo of the melody is
justified by the line: for the preceding initial motive, which itself
varies that of the main theme, no longer rises, but sinks from its
climactic first note B onwards, and this falling makes use of the in-

terval relationships of the joker motive. In this way, in the first variant, strengthening and weakening tendencies act against each other.
The second, two measures later, brings about their resolution in a
clearly increasing intensity. The harmonic shift is intensified by the
tonally alien bass note B-flat, a powerful neighbor degree. The melody, however, in which the immediately preceding figure still rever-
berates, again rises, to F, yet falls short of the F-sharp of the
beginning. So that no abrupt violence is done, this version is repeated on the next appearance of the motive,[8] only minimally
changed by a harmonic alteration. Two measures later[9] it is confirmed, now further reinforced harmonically by more emphatic deviations from the basic key and a melodic version of the sixteenth
notes that, over a diminished seventh chord, touches A, a third
higher than the original figure. Toward the end of the exposition of
the main theme, therefore, the motive makes its freshest impression
horizontally and vertically, only to dissolve away in accompanying
voices up to the beginning of the transition. The adventures that be-
fall it in the development are possibly not surprising, given the
usual nature of such selections. But the specifically Mahlerian variant technique is continued in the recapitulation. The improvising
expansion of the themes from the development re-echoes in their
formulation in the recapitulation. Where the joker motive reappears
openly in the recapitulation,[10] although the harmonization of the
second variant with B-flat in the bass is used, a harmonization that
has to an extent superseded the earlier figures, the melody soars a
seventh to D, a fourth above the previous high point of the motive
and, in its reaffirmation two measures later with only a slight
change in harmony, to the high F. The weakening represented in the
exposition by the fall from F-sharp to E and F, then an octave lower,
is as if made good. In the coda of the movement, finally, the motive,
carefully prepared melodically and with a new harmonization,[11] is
brought to its absolute climax, an A, exactly an octave above the one
that the motive had provisionally attained toward the end of the exposition of the main theme. So rational are Mahler's irrationalities.
With increasing experience the variant technique becomes more and
more precise. In the late works it often concentrates on critical notes
within a theme or even a motive. The very feature that is striking in

a melodic unit is modified. The minor theme in the first movement of the Ninth Symphony, for example, contains a G-sharp not belonging to the key,[12] which determines in itself the dissonant character of the whole complex; this very G-sharp, however, or its equivalent, is then replaced on many occasions by an A, i.e. a perfect fifth above the tonic of D minor. Ratz, in his analysis, has shown in detail the formal function of this change of the two critical notes.[13] In a similar way the chromatic linking motive[14] scattered over the whole movement is later subjected to a variant in which the critical whole-tone step to the last element of the motive, from E to F-sharp, is widened to the minor third E–G. Thereby the motive surrenders its acid quality, as the whole recapitulation demands, to merge finally with the core of the coda.[15]

Traditionally, musical subcomplexes were seen as the resultants of the tension between the preordained categories, particularly tonality, and the singular composing impulse. Both were mediated through each other—the details partly the product of tonal relations, the tonality confirmed or restored by the individual impulses. Form, however, in the narrower sense of music theory, that is, the great architecture within time, had long remained outside this interplay. Either the specific life of the composition was trimmed willynilly to fit the prescribed categories, or the individual impulses asserted their autonomy and used the form only as a vehicle. Mahler at last restores the reciprocity. He translates it to the formal organization as a whole. The latter does not ignore the traditional architecture. On occasion, as in the first movement of the Sixth Symphony, which originally had repeat marks after the exposition, it is acknowledged in very expansive music; yet it is filled even here with largely unschematic material: for example, a chorale serves as a transition. Even what can be strictly related to the sonata model has its individual law of motion. Thus, in the Finale of the Sixth, after an introduction not only very extensive but already heavy with symphonic impetus, and after the towering development, an insistently symmetrical recapitulation was impermissible. To the extent that the sense of form expects symmetries, they are provided by the rondo-like return of the introduction. Among constant variants of strict modulatory function within the progress of the whole, it is the relatively static element. On the other hand, the oversized complexes demand, after the use of the tonality proper to them, a compensation, a homeostasis of the construction. For its sake Mahler concedes a kind of recapitulation after all. But this takes account of what has gone before by partially inverting the sequence of the main complexes. The movement, which traverses immeasurable intervals of time, succeeds in squaring the circle: it is dynamic and tectonic in one, without one principle annulling the other. The recapitulation begins with its second theme complex, yet is not set apart, merging with the introduction.[16] This is appropriate because at its beginning, as if under glass, the chief motives of the second theme complex have been displayed. In the meantime all those motives, to use an expression current in 1900, have found fulfillment. From their pre-existence the real symphonic existence has come into being. The second theme complex, through appearing now as if in the framework of an extended introduction, is kept outside the actual relatively faithful recapitulation, neither ruminated upon nor neglected. The recapitulation must make do with the first theme complex and is disposed of briefly, again without a pause. Once again, in a procedure similar to that in the development of the first movement of the Fourth Symphony, it is not separated from what went before, the musical flow passing unnoticed into it.[17] Once the whole has gathered impetus, the caesuras become smaller than at first: symphonic flow repudiates symphonic formalism. Mahler would rather disregard topographic clarity, and smoothen originally sharp contours, than contravene the rigor of an inner sense of form. He artfully withdraws the recapitulation, which he needs, from the surface of perception. This endows it, in the Finale of the Sixth, with an expression of sketchy ghostliness reminiscent of "Rewelge." The recapitulation becomes an apparition; the character legitimizes the remaining symmetry. Not only here, in Mahler, do sections of emphatic, bodily presence in the music alternate with such spectral episodes. Many movements develop in order to seize or relinquish their own reality; music should be entirely present only as the result of its own enactment. The novel-subject, which in the music seeks the world, nevertheless fails to be at one with it. It hopes for salvation from passing over into the very reality from which it shrank; it seeks this reality in its own inner movement. What remains unmentioned in the second exposition complex of the Finale is then fleetingly reiterated, the coda too being extremely brief. The recapitulation was the crux of sonata form. It revokes what since Beethoven had been the decisive element, the dynamic of the development, in a way comparable to the effect of a film on a spectator who stays in his seat at the end and watches the beginning again. Beethoven mastered this by a tour de force that became a rule with him: at the fertile moment at the beginning of the recapitulation he presents the result of the dynamic, the evolution as the affirmation and justification of what has been, what was there in any case. That is his complicity with the guilt of the great idealistic systems, with the dialectician Hegel, for whom in the end the essential character of negations, and so of becoming, amounted to a theodicy of being. In the recapitulation, music, as a ritual of bourgeois freedom, remained, like the society in which it is and which is in it, enslaved to mythical unfreedom. It manipulates the natural relationship circling within it as if what recurs, by virtue of its mere recurrence, were more than it is, were metaphysical meaning itself, the "Idea." Conversely, however, music without the recapitulation takes on a disproportional, abrupt aspect that is unsatisfying in not merely a shallow sense: as if it lacked something, had no end. And indeed, all new music is tormented by the question of how it can close, not merely end, now that concluding cadences, which themselves have something of the nature of the recapitulation, no longer suffice— the recapitulation being, one might say, merely the application of the cadence formula on a large scale. Mahler's arrival at this choice converges, however, with that of the greatest novels of his generation. Where he repeats past material for formal reasons, he does not sing its praises or those of transience itself. Through the variant his music remembers things past and half-forgotten from a great distance, protests against their absolute fruitlessness and yet pronounces the past ephemeral, irrecoverable. The music's immanent idea resides in such redeeming fidelity.

Mahler's critique of ready-made patterns transforms the sonata principle. Not only in the Sixth, but often—in the First, Third,

Fourth, and Seventh—the expositions are strikingly brief. The model for this tendency, which complements the expansion of the development, is the *Eroica*. In Mahler such brevity opposes music's architectonic quality. The less he strives for static correspondences, the less extensively he needs to treat the complexes that might have corresponded; but what now has to represent architectonic identity becomes obtrusive through its brevity. Within the principle of permanent modification the development gains preponderance, but it no longer functions as a dynamic antithesis to static basic relationships. The sonata principle is thereby changed in its innermost part. The expositions, previously structures with substantial weight of their own, become expositions in the modest sense of presentations of the dramatis personae, whose musical story is then told. When Mahler, in the Ninth Symphony, probably as a result of his experiences with *Das Lied von der Erde*, abandoned the sonata principle, he merely manifested overtly what had been prepared subcutaneously by his whole work. His extensive time consciousness demands sections that emerge from each other. Their tension, which in its rise and fall surpasses that of earlier symphonies, is produced by the proportions of the parts, not through intensification. Mahler's oeuvre as a whole stands apart from the sonata principle as something disparate. In the First Symphony the short exposition is monothematic, the orthodox lyrical theme being absent. In general Mahler tends to formulate the second theme complexes briefly. According to Romantic practice, his "song" themes take from song their closed melody, always more or less complete in itself; its formal function in the evolution of the piece is its relatively static nature. But what for the time being is merely there can usually be stated directly and succinctly. If the upper-part melodies of the themes of second theme groups were prolonged and savored, they would push aside the symphonic totality. In the Third Symphony the sonata principle is disempowered, the introduction, exposition of the first theme, and development being disproportionate by its criteria. The first movement of the Fourth, admittedly, is a sonata, yet archaistically, as was once the first movement of Beethoven's Eighth; the second theme would be an instrumental song far too self-sufficient for a sonata as such; in addition, for all its terseness, the closing section is more like a third theme, far removed from what has preceded it. Only retrospectively do the contrasting ideas become a ramifying unity in the development, the first one in Mahler that develops the components of the exposition in an explicating way: with it the movement truly begins as a story. After the orthodox recapitulation the coda completes what the former has omitted at its beginning. Despite all this, however, this movement also opposes sonata form, not only because everything is composed within quotation marks—because the music says: Once upon a time there was a sonata—but also technically. The exposition complexes differ so much, and are so energetically divided, that they are incapable from the outset of being contracted into a verdict. The Fifth Symphony comes to terms with the idea of sonata form by splitting, in a sense, into two first movements; by its spirit the first would be the exposition, the second the development. The exposition movement is a funeral march arranged in squares, without free space for development; the second is constructed as a sonata rondo with its own development; the extensive interpolations from the first movement confuse the sonata feeling. If the Fifth tends toward the spirit of the sonata, it resists its structure all the more irritably. This is only confronted in the first movement of the Sixth Symphony. Admittedly, in it, too, the complex of themes is very compressed and the much-reviled main melody from it is only just indicated in the recapitulation. The structure of the movement might well have been suggested by a notion of the tragic that Mahler's weltschmerz accepted from the aesthetic of the day, without at that stage measuring it against his own formal intention. His self-criticism may temporarily have judged the highly original, eccentric procedure of the first three symphonies irresponsibly lax. He used the traditional sonata form to discipline himself. In straining to meet its demands, he gained mastery of open-work thematic procedure, the fine-spun texture. The craft of the mature works helped to spiritualize them. Mahler retained these acquisitions when he was free enough to jettison the impeding conditions he had imposed on himself since the Fourth. Moreover, the sonata skeleton is indispensable to the last movement of the Sixth in binding together its dimensions: the intensification of expansive power in it needs to be complemented by a capacity for imposing order. In the consciousness of his complete technical mastery he dares to undertake a work of the Beethovenian type. In any case, epic composition was never the mere antithesis of the dramatic but also close to it, like the novel, in its onward momentum, its tensions and explosions. Now Mahler pays tribute to the drama in a sonata form that he constructs with paradigmatic firmness as first theme, transition, second theme, and closing group. Tragedy refuses a nominalistic form. The totality that sanctions for its own glory the destruction of the individual, who has no choice but to be destroyed, rules unchallenged. Mahler's emancipation from sonata form was mediated by the sonata. He absorbed its idea in the middle symphonies, to arrive finally at a mode of composition in which each measure was equally close to the center.

Large-scale form is the declared concern in the Finale of the Sixth Symphony, with the first movement of the Third Mahler's longest instrumental piece. Its formal idea differs from that of the earlier work in that epic expansion attains tightest control of itself: in this sense the movement is the center of Mahler's entire oeuvre. The polyphony of the Fifth Symphony is adjourned; the temporal dimensions would have been incompatible with contrapuntal attention to the simultaneous. Its place is taken by a no less closely successive form of connection through thematic and motivic working-out of extreme richness. To this the material is predisposed behind the scenes. Between the two main complexes there are, despite their Mahlerian terseness, countless cross-connections, above all through the interval of a second and the dotted rhythm; at the beginning of the recapitulation of the first theme they are presented in counterpoint. In keeping with its emphatic basic character, the movement is a sonata finale, not a rondo. The long introduction, beginning four times on different levels, not only serves to articulate the whole, but is later integrated with the Allegro. It immediately presents the Allegro's chief motives, while some of its specific themes, like the sombre chorale,[18] whose prayer is not granted, are themselves developed. The first theme does not, in the traditional way, follow directly from the introduction, there being a short allegro moderato transition modulating from the initial key of C minor to the principal key of A minor; later Mahler recalls this transitional version of the first theme in one of the most important ideas (*Modelle*) in the development.[19] The first complex of the exposition proper[20] is an energetic march. It is continued by a "deployment"[21] of the brass related to the chorale of the introduction and accompanied by the traditional eighth-note movement, which opens into a field of dissolution. The second theme complex begins with a distinct jolt into D major;[22] it too is intentionally brief, but in its rapid upsurge probably the most novel-like constellation anywhere in Mahler, dancing like an imperiled boat in choppy water. Without being ashamed of the simple sequences of its consequent phrase, this asymmetrical theme, purified of continuous movement, is unfathomable in its expressiveness. It changes iridescently between careless joy and surging intoxication. It is helped in this by its structure. Like prose, it strings together heterogeneous components, above all widely separated rhythmical values, which are nevertheless, by virtue of their harmonic links, organically intertwined. Here, as elsewhere in Mahler, one might speak of village passages, as distinct from the too-straight roads that are traditionally understood as obligatory for the symphony. At the same time the theme's complex form enables it to be utilized equally well as a unity, to be selected and spun out like an individual component, and, above all, allows all the subterranean connections between its motives to be exploited. What is forgone, after the graphic dualism of the first and second themes, is a more extensive closing section or a third theme. The development again begins, after an abbreviated allusion to the introductory complex,[23] with a modulatory jolt, harsher this time than at the beginning of the second theme complex: in this way great novelists like Jacobsen were apt to omit whole periods of the lives of their heroes, lighting up critical phases with abrupt resolve; what Jacobsen selected expressly as a principle of "bad composition"[24] becomes, in Mahler's great formal experiment as well, one of good writing. The immense development, truly here the symphony proper, was to be constructed in such a way that it becomes neither incongruous with what has gone before, nor entangled in itself. For this, the improvising freedom that adopts the pattern of the development as a corrective is not enough. That freedom is only sanctioned in that each main section, which very precisely develops its models, soars expansively towards its end, as if its own progress had loosened the constraint; such a parallelism of disintegration fields unifies the diversity of characters to exactly the same extent as it softens the matter restrained; the great rhythm of the development becomes itself one of necessity and freedom. Each exertion is, in a sense, rewarded. Even the path to freedom is not a nature reserve. Precisely where the passage is thoroughly in motion, it obeys rigorous construction. The development is sharply divided, like that in the first movement of the Third, into four parts. The first[25] is a free variant of the second theme complex of the exposition. It compensates for the latter's brevity and forms the bridge between development and exposition, as if it were a retrospective recapitulation. The tendency toward retrospectiveness exerts a continuing effect until the actual recapitulation much later. The first part of the development is supported primarily by the passionate consequent phrase of the second theme.[26] The beginning of the second is recognizable by the first hammer blow.[27] In the manner of the overall retrograde construction—Berg loved this form later—the main theme is not yet introduced. Rather, the second sector has the main theme's entry-like continuation as its subject, and explicates its relation both to the introduction and to the second theme complex. At the end it heightens a reminiscence of the main march in the exposition,[28] with its fanfare-like ostinati in the winds and chains of trills, to the point of barbaric ferocity, clattering as the *Holzklapper* had done previously.[29] The general rest[30] at this point has its thematic model in a eighth-note rest in the exposition.[31] Before the third part of the development,[32] this caesura gives breathing space in the otherwise over-dense mesh, the tension leads on to a colon, like that in a march introduction, so that the interruption only heightens the expectation, which then is fulfilled in the great march, the third, central part of the development. In the spirit of the sonata the motivic nucleus of the main theme is worked out, but as something evolving, not firmly congealed. The dynamic of the compositional character communicates itself to the compositional procedure; in an unregulated way the rule is still followed. The flow of what is only now evolving without resistance does not allow the development, even in the critical part at its center, to falter for a second. Its broadly flowing end would be architectonically the equivalent, for example, of the close of the first part of the development. At the beginning of the fourth and last there is again a hammer blow.[33] This part corresponds visibly to the second, as a kind of chorale-like elaboration of the continuation theme from the first exposition complex. The great march is installed between the concrete piers of the wind theme. Thanks to its affinity with the introduction, it joins seamlessly with the latter's full return. However, the correspondence between the second and fourth parts of the development is not a mechanical one: the latter varies the former in intensified form. The Brucknerian potential for perspectives glimpsed through the center of the development is fulfilled for the first time here. Constructively, the correspondence between the second and fourth sections ensures that the great march, being inserted between firm elements, for all its expansive power does not inundate the whole, but retains within the totality of the development the relative weight of a part. That expansive power, to be sure, has exhausted itself in the development. After the reordered recapitulation, the introduction,[34] on its last appearance, is only lightly touched upon; a coda closes swiftly with the black sound of the trombone. The inspiration in the Finale of the Sixth is its formal idea, not the individual themes composed with this idea in view. The content of the piece is brought about by its grandiose immanence of form. The insatiably ecstatic intensification of the feeling of living consumes itself. The liftings up are those prior to the fall into that darkness that only entirely fills the musical space in the last bars. Through pure musical intensity what takes place in the movement becomes one with its own negation.

The first movement of the Seventh is closely related to the outer movements of the Sixth. But Mahler's capacity to renew symphonic types from within themselves is not confined to after-echoes. Through a changed illumination the whole movement becomes a variant. It translates the attainments of the preceding orchestral symphonies into the image-world of the early Mahler; in view of the predominant chiaroscuro effects the trite epithet of a Romantic symphony is excusable. Despite the most emphatic construction the movement is sensuously more colorful than anything previously written by Mahler; his late style goes back to it. The major is resplendent with added notes, as a kind of super-major,[35] as in the famous chord from the Adagio of Bruckner's Ninth.[36] The contrasts, including those of sound, are deepened, as is the perspective; even the wind chorus is toned down as compared to its previous appearance, for example, through opposing the tenor horn and solo trombones. Exploitation of the shared thirds allows chords originally located far apart to follow each other according to diatonic rules.[37] All in all, the harmonic resources are noticeably increased. Horizontal and vertical fourth-formations may, with peculiarities of the thematic formulation, have directly influenced Schoenberg's First Chamber Symphony, composed a year later. As in the young Schoenberg, the expanded harmony becomes constructive. Cadences still fresh reinforce the awareness of tonality; on many occasions in the movement the cadences give an impression of closure.[38] Still more than in the Sixth, the first part of the development corresponds to a rudimentary variant of the exposition, freely writing out the conventional exposition repeat. This leads into a long, extraneous, frequently interrupted episodic section. What sounds after it like the beginning of the central development,[39] launched with a Beethovenian gesture, stays under the persistent sway of the episode passages, like the second movement of the Fifth; the actual developmental parts are extremely succinct. Mahler's epic intention experiments with the technique acquired in the Sixth Symphony: the development is split into two elements hostile to sonata form, an exposition variant and an episode field referring back, through the expansion of motives, to the introduction, this field finally issuing in the recapitulation of the introduction; the qualitatively different becomes entirely immanent to the composition. The recapitulation is intensified as compared to the exposition, but in accordance with correct practice. The shadow of the Sixth, in which the movement exists, then becomes the realm of shadows of the three middle movements. Vanished is the tragic aspiration of the Sixth. It is banished probably less by that ominously positive element that, to be sure, ruins the Finale, than by a half-consciousness that the category of the tragic cannot be reconciled with the epic ideal of a music open in time. Having mastered totality, the composition turns its thoughts to the opposite, a meaning that arises from fragments.

Mahler's nominalism, his critique of forms by means of the specific impulse, also draws into itself the type of movement, a legacy of the suit, that had survived most tenaciously since Haydn, the minuet and scherzo; only in Mendelssohn was it reconsidered. The *Ländler* in Mahler's First is still traditional through its orientation toward Bruckner, not only in the nature of its themes but in the coarsely disjunct planes, each of which, however, has its own static harmony; the trio has a harmonic richness and finesse[40] that is not taken in by the stylistic model of the rustic dance. The Viennese tenderness of that trio recurs in the second *Nachtmusik* of the Seventh and, from far off, in *Das Lied von der Erde;* already the phrase endings are allowed to fall in resignation.[41] If the waltz from *Der Freischütz,* above all its disintegration into fragments toward the end, has something Mahlerian about it, the First acknowledges it by quotation.[42] The scherzos of the Second and Third, both songs reinterpreted and enlarged symphonically, fuse the scherzo type with that of the strophic ballade, which they set in motion for the first time; through inserting unrepeated and unrepeatable fields, they seek an escape from the monotony of the dance's spinning. The Scherzo of the Fourth precisely sums up the results of those of the preceding symphonies. However, when Mahler had behind him spotless achievement, he nervously avoided looking back at it. His critical concern draws this form, curiously resistant to historical influences, inexorably into the force field of symphonic composition. With an exertion that he himself[43] must have felt as extraordinary, he conceives in the Fifth the novelty of the development-scherzo. To be sure, the scherzo section and the first trio—more replete with characters, however, than any previously found within this pattern— are at first clearly set out, but with a dovetailing that allows them to intermesh. Their stiffly formal nature is made dynamic without the ground plan being obscured, a true masterpiece. In it Mahlerian polyphony has one of its origins. Because the scherzo dances remain as clearly delineated as they must also interpenetrate, he combines them simultaneously, mingling the scherzo themes contrapuntally. The coda, with four concurrent themes,[44] goes furthest in this. These artifices are in no way playful: they alone master the abundance of the dance figures without curtailing it. The structure of the

movement—without which, incidentally, Strauss's *Rosenkavalier*
would hardly be thinkable—is itself governed by counterpoint. The
successive themes stand out against each other like good counterpoints to a *cantus firmus*. The orchestral mastery is revealed in
small traits. At the very beginning the counter melody of the clarinets and bassoons is so placed that it becomes entirely distinct, not
dull or feeble, as one fears on a mere reading. This full manner of
composing has implications beyond itself; in one place the pure two-
part counterpoint of obligato horn and first violins first draws the
richness of the full orchestra with it.[45] The end of the main section
of the Scherzo,[46] which resembles a closing section or an *Abgesang*,
becomes what it is through the economy principle; this section in-
verts the main line. A remembrance of something never heard before is the pizzicato episode,[47] the archetype of the shadowy in
Mahler; the *schüchtern* (timid) oboe entry that follows it[48] has the
ineffability of a voice venturing as a living being among shades. In
harsh contrast to this Scherzo is that of the Sixth. If the Scherzo of
the Fifth labors at the possibility of a symphonic unity arising from
dances arranged serially as in a suite, that of the Sixth, bracketed in
terms of motives and harmony between the outer movements, asks
how, from a minimum of initial materials, a maximum of changing
characters is to be distilled. The Scherzo and trio draw together; a
variant of the trio theme, undisguised in its ductus, appears at the
very beginning of the first exposition of the Scherzo.[49] The contra-
vention of the rules reinforces the unity at which the movement
aims; if later the trio, entitled *altväterlich* (antiquated), adopts an
ancestrally dignified gait, it finds itself in uncomfortable proximity
to the Scherzo section, as in a nightmare. The unity, which leaves
nothing out, is itself intended to form a character, to establish that
tormenting insistence that preludes the stiff, intentionally dragging
theme of the Scherzo. Such rigidity is found in too many themes in
the whole Sixth Symphony for it to be attributed to a wearying of
melodic invention: it has the same implacable quality as strict sonata form. The threatening, asphyxiating effect produced by the
Scherzo undoubtedly results from Mahler's singular procedure.
Not everywhere, however, is his strenuous economy secure from
unintentional monotony. Only the final coda attains an authen-

ticity in which all's ill that ends ill. The Scherzo of the Seventh is
again a development-scherzo like that of the Fifth, yet reduced by
the need to represent a third character piece between the two *Nachtmusik*. The trio, only lightly sketched and interrupted, speaking
with a voice almost more touching than anything else in Mahler,
literally becomes the victim of symphonic development, brutally
distorted as was once Berlioz's idée fixe of the beloved in the desolate
Finale,[50] only to recover its beauty in a consequent phrase of dignified composure.[51]

The antagonism within Mahler's technique between a repetition-shunning fullness on one hand and a densely interwoven, advancing totality on the other not only concerns the form in the narrower sense of the successive complexes, but informs every dimension of his composition. For Mahler uses each of them equally to realize his intention; his work is a preliminary stage of the integral art-work. They support each other, one compensating weaknesses in the other. Paul Bekker—perhaps oversensitive to the fervent, grieving tone of its melody, reminiscent of the *Kindertotenlieder*—has criticized the triviality of the main theme of the Andante of the Sixth Symphony, which later soars magnificently toward fulfillment. Yet its powerful cantabile quality may not have satisfied Mahler himself. He therefore so arranged the ten-measure theme metrically as to produce ambivalences between the ends and beginnings of phrases. The repetition of the opening idea falls on the third beat instead of the first, and so on a relatively weak part of the measure; metrical irregularity is the dowry which folksong-like melodies bring with them to symphonic prose. In the ingenious Scherzo of the Fourth the stress of a main rhythmic shape displaces itself by an eighth note.[1] Mahler's use of rhythm is a delicate and favored means of his technique of variants. With constant increases and diminutions he preserves the melodic unity intact in the agogically simplest way, while still modifying it. The *Kindertotenlieder* are particularly rich in such formations. Thanks to arrangements of this kind, Mahler's themes lose the trace of banality that someone so disposed could criticize in some successions of intervals; usually in Mahler the charge of banality dogmatically isolates individual dimensions, blind to the fact that in him character, "originality," are defined not by single dimensions but only by their relationships to each other. That Mahler's procedure is exempted by its multidimensionality from the reproach of banality in no way denies the existence of banal elements or their function in the construction of the whole. What artifices such as these metrical devices bring about in banal musical material is the very refraction that integrates the banal into the art-work, which needs it as an autonomous agent, as an element of immediacy in the musical totality. Even the category of the banal is dynamic in Mahler; it appears in order to be paralyzed, not dissolved in the musical process without residue. This process is the opposed force imparting discipline—in brief, Mahler's "technique." The concern for realization is expressed, in face of the music's abundance, in the demand for clarity in all strata. So well did the great conductor know the limitations of the orchestra, and of other conductors too, that he foresaw all the havoc they wreak through slovenliness, deficient understanding, lack of time, or under the pressure of the musical fabric of his works. The expression marks, like many peculiarities of the instrumentation in the mature works, are protective measures against the performers. The inevitable breach between the music itself and its adequate reproduction is registered by the former: Mahler attempted to achieve a foolproof composition. His wisdom, no less than that of the "Fischpredigt," is confirmed by the fact that the very mistakes he tried to prevent occur again and again; for example, eminent conductors invariably speed up where the score warns against it. Concern for correct reproduction became a canon of the composition. To compose music in such a way that the performance cannot destroy it, and so virtually to abolish performance, means to compose with absolute clarity and unambiguity. Because nothing can be blurred, novelesque fullness is subordinated to appraising economy, as in Berg. Mahler attains maximum effects with a minimum of means. Even in his most excessive work, the Third, a turning point in the Minuet sounds as if an immense shudder has run through the music,[2] yet without the use of a tutti; the solo-like sound of the minuet complex is enough. Instrumentally, the effect is attributable to details previously avoided, such as the entry of the four horns, the chords in the harps, and the simple forte of the strings. For the first time the violins entirely hold the foreground, so that for a moment the composition is turned fully outwards, whereas up to now it has been vegetating inwardly. The true reason for the effect, however, as of every one that is more than a mere effect, may well be contained in the composition itself, the very bright sound with suspension of A–E–B–D–G and the following dominant minor ninth chord. Mahler's typical mode of composition—the tripartite division into melody, accompanying voices, and bass; the tendency toward three-part counterpoint obscured by doublings and superimposed chords, so unlike the usual form of orchestral polyphony—seeks to clarify the successive abundance by a simple presentation of the simultaneous. From the Fifth Symphony on, through the technique of motivic combination, the composition also becomes richer and denser.

The increasing integration of Mahler's procedure as a composer does not, as often happen after him, devalue the individual dimensions but rather throws them into relief; the whole retroactively invigorates the elements that brought it about. In the early Mahler, the harmony, while possessing properties of its own, was not yet an autonomous medium. Only where other elements, like melody and metrics, become specific do they enrich harmony with dissonant arpeggios and degrees. As early as the Third Symphony there are, as in the Funeral March of the Fifth, molten chords with a complex life of their own, as quite early in the introduction.[3] A recitative-like voice in the basses collides with the harmony proper; whenever this happens in the Third, irregular sounds continue to occur.[4] In the conflict between sustaining harmonies and emancipated single voices, as later in the New Music, the vertical sound is brought into being by counterpoint. The loveliest example of the interdependence of melody and harmony in the young Mahler was pointed out by Alban Berg—the central section sung by the girl in "Der Schildwache Nachtlied," where an arching phrase with wide intervals and a rhythm alternating between double and triple meter mirror each other in chord progressions and sonorities having a bodily depth, such as the one with the clashing notes C–B–D♯–F♯–D,[5] which, because it is derived from part-writing, does not impair the harmonic texture. No less beautiful is the variant on it in the coda, which preserves its dissonant character in totally changed chords and at the end, with a sharply dissonant construction of the dominant seventh chord of B-flat major—a D instead of a C—opens into wide spaces.[6] In the mature Mahler such harmonic *trouvailles* become more frequent. They mold the form through perspective. Thus the harmonizations of the second themes of the first movements of the Sixth and, above all, the Seventh attain effects of depth that influence the themes more than does momentary inspiration, as elements of the whole process; as this happens the harmony itself becomes heartbreaking as it has been before only occasionally in Schubert. In this manner Mahler harmonizes, above all, corner points, thematic hinges, where the harmonization rends open a third dimension that relates the two-dimensional melodic surfaces in the foreground to the total symphonic volume. The once audacious sonority of such passages, particularly in the Seventh,[7] has meanwhile gained acceptance even at the commodity level of ballet and light music. In Mahler, however, they do not merely add spice but, as composedout degrees of the scale, clarify the meaning, the melodic seriousness, then the flow of the form. Such expediency even enhances their beauty, keeping it young, like the similarly intended fortissimo chords at the climax of the last orchestral piece from Schoenberg's op. 16. Free and dissonant harmonization, in the Seventh, gives rise to large and dissonant intervals in the melodic line as well, incomparably in Berg's favorite passage from the second *Nachtmusik*, a tenderly melancholy moment that the solo violin, the second violins, and the solo viola take from each other[8] as if they were plucking the leaves from chords; such interaction between vertical and horizontal is anachronistically modern, although modernity up to now has evolved nothing comparable.

Like Mahler's harmony, his counterpoint was invigorated by the denser symphonic texture. Mahler only turned his attention to it in the Fourth, incorporating it as a dimension of composition in the

Fifth and later. To be sure, he seldom sustains counterpoint through whole movements, usually only in sections that derive their character from it. His first movement of sustained polyphonic pretensions, the second of the Fifth Symphony, contrastingly continues to treat the long interpolations from the first movement homophonically, as if the pressure of the contrapuntal music had become unbearable to the point of rupture. However, the following movement, the great Scherzo, is contrapuntal throughout. This whirling, agitated piece, a waltz enlarged to a symphony, has its great caesura,[9] the moment of suspension. Yet the sudden apparition does not remain outside, but evolves into a second trio. While it never quite relinquishes the quality of differentness, its themes are nevertheless assimilated to the symphonic whole; in the recapitulation, directly before the coda, it is repeated complete with caesura in abbreviated form.[10] The contrapuntal arrangement of the movement as a whole technically compels everything that becomes caught up in the music to be an intrinsic part of it; the unity of the polyphonic structure resists anything not subject to its law. Extraneous material, on the other hand, is more possible the looser the composition. Mahler's attitude to counterpoint is divided. At the Vienna Conservatory he was, curiously enough, released from the study of counterpoint on the basis of his own compositions from his student days. According to Natalie Bauer-Lechner, he later regretted this:

as far back as I can remember my musical thinking was, oddly enough, never anything but polyphonic. But here I'm probably still suffering from lack of strict counterpoint, which every student who has been trained in it would use at this point with the greatest of ease.[11] . . . Now I understand why, as we are told, Schubert still wanted to study counterpoint even shortly before his death. He was aware of what he lacked. And I can feel for him in this, as I am myself deficient in this technique, having missed a really thorough grounding in counterpoint in my student years. Admittedly, intellect makes up for it in my case, but the expenditure of energy needed for this is out of all proportion.[12]

The appeal to "intellect" indicates that despite the assertion of his primarily polyphonic thinking, he experienced counterpoint as something mediated; this is supported by the homophony of the first three symphonies. By polyphony he obviously means the tendency toward chaotic, unorganized sound, the unregulated, fortuitous simultaneity of the "world," the echo of which his music, through its artistic organization, seeks to become. What he loved in polyphony was that which gave offense to the "pedantry" of which Mahler's brother-in-law, Arnold Rosé, once spoke; in Mahler's youth counterpoint was still part of its domain. Light is thrown on this aspect by a passage in Bauer-Lechner, which could hardly have been invented:

> The following Sunday, we went on the same walk with Mahler. At the fête on the Kreuzberg, an even worse witches' sabbath was in progress. Not only were innumerable barrel-organs blaring out from merry-go-rounds, swings, shooting galleries and puppet shows, but a military band and a men's choral society had established themselves there as well. All these groups, in the same forest clearing, were creating an incredible musical pandemonium without paying the slightest attention to each other. Mahler exclaimed: "You hear? That's polyphony, and that's where I get it from! Even when I was quite a small child, in the woods at Iglau, this sort of thing used to move me strangely, and impressed itself upon me. For it's all the same whether heard in a din like this or in the singing of thousands of birds; in the howling of the storm, the lapping of the waves, or the crackling of the fire. Just in this way—from quite different directions—must the themes appear; and they must be just as different from each other in rhythm and melodic character (everything else is merely many-voiced writing, homophony in disguise). The only difference is that the artist orders and unites them all into one concordant and harmonious whole."[13]

Counterpoint for Mahler was the self-alienated form of music that imposed itself on the subject, in the extreme case mere simultaneous sounds. Fugue at first seemed by its nature comical to him, and some such suspicion ought to keep polyphonic thought on the alert, if it is not to lapse after Mahler into heteronomy. But he absorbed counterpoint, like everything alienated, to the exact extent that the multiple sounds overflow thematic unity. His multiplicity is itself a principle of organization, of what Mahler called "order" (*Ordnung*). The interweaving of the voices, that integration of music that omits nothing, flooding the whole musical space and inhumanly expelling the potential listener from the music, seems to him at first a metaphor for an inescapable and stifling net of functional connections. Instead of with the perpetual motion of the movements of the symphonies of his youth, Mahler's concern now is with the elaboration of voices that emerge, are juxtaposed, and vanish again. Their density grows more inexorable, but also, through the appeal of their logic, less meaningless than the monotonous, uninterrupted motion within which nothing happens. Before the plenitude of figures within such immanence the mere fanfare, as an allegory of that which is remote to it, must be as inadequate spiritually as it remained musically powerless. The more closely related technique and content become in the composition, the less crudely is the world of images polarized. If polyphony is suggested by the idea of the world's course, at the same time, as a condition of the truth of music, it reinforces music's autonomy: "Where id is, ego shall be."

Through such autonomy Mahler's counterpoint is distinguished from the New German version of his time, whether of Strauss or Reger: through clarity. Filling-in remains filling-in, harmonic *sans phrase*; voices, even subsidiary ones, are fully worked out as melodies; Mahler does not write hybrid filling voices, nor inexact arabesques buzzing in accompaniment. He is allergic to pseudo-counterpoint, which in reality merely duplicates the harmonic progression. Rather than feigning polyphony for the sake of richness of sound, he accepts occasional meagerness of composition. The first specifically Mahlerian counterpoint is the spiky oboe melody that is set against the canon in the third movement of the First:[14] the program for Mahler's tone. Such counterpoint has a directly characterizing intention. The caustic characters accord well with the technical need to complement the quasi-folksong melodies by others that differ from them to markedly, almost like negations.

The distinguishing definition of themes becomes in many cases absolute, embracing their autonomous nature; character is simply difference. Nevertheless, Mahler seldom wrote a constructively binding, multiple counterpoint, seldom uses polyphony to create the acoustic space.[15] Where he goes so far, in the Scherzo of the Fifth, in complexes of its Finale, in the first movement of the Eighth, he is influenced by principles of stylization—often the fugato—although in the Burlesque of the Ninth Symphony the reason is directly compositional. As is the caricaturing "Lob des hohen Verstandes," even for the late Mahler multiple counterpoint still bore the odium of shoolteacherish narrow-mindedness; hardly by accident is the entirely contrapuntal movement of the Ninth entitled "Burlesque" and dedicated to "my brothers in Apollo," as if, with these earnest striving souls, the nature of fugue were also to be ridiculed; the suspension field is homophonic. Like musical classicism, and certainly like *Die Meistersinger*, Mahler still often associates counterpoint with humor and play; the serious for him is the free, autonomous life of form. Yet in play the polyphonic need already arises: play seeks release in construction. In late Mahler counterpoint rebels. All in all, his counterpoint seeks a manner that is terse and free at once. It is probably the most decisive element he owed to folk music. For him, writing counterpoint was to invent for one melody another that is no less a melody yet neither too closely resembles nor obliterates the first. This may have been how rural polyphonic improvisations on songs were executed; Mahler may have had in mind the *Überschlag* from the Austrian Alps, which Berg was to include expressly in the Violin Concerto in homage to Mahler, the second melody simultaneously added to a first according to harmonic rules, which is its shadow yet is melodious in itself. The only difference is that Mahler's free counterpoints, with increasing maturity, move further and further away from the *Überschlag*'s dependence on its melody, even when they are used in stylized dances.[16] In the invention of such counterpoints Mahler's imagination was inexhaustible. In counterpoint too he thinks in variants. The superimposed voices constantly enrich the composition, each recapitulation of a form-complex being made by them into something different, although its core is not affected. The cello

melody in the slow movement of the Second Symphony was understood in this way, being, moreover, in double counterpoint with the
main theme, the slow *Ländler*. The earliest *Überschlag*-like figures
in Mahler, in the second movement of the First Symphony,[17] are
Brucknerian; through their type of superimposed polyphony
Mahler gradually became a master of free counterpoint. Structurally, this technique responds to a limitation: that in Mahler the
truly melodic voices always rise above a lower element with a harmonic function, whether a bass or sustaining lower parts; given that
harmony still held primacy in his work, the upper and lower parts
cannot be exchanged as freely as in Schoenberg. What this tonal
limit costs Mahler in terms of the thematic concision of polyphony
he compensates by its spontaneity. As free counterpoint has its origin in the *Überschlag*, Mahler's much-noticed tendency toward
bass-lessness is derived from dance music, the alternation of tonic
and dominant in the bass instead of a proper bass line. Mahler's approach translates this into a peculiar suspendedness of the music in
mid-air, a further heresy against the official logic of harmony. The
vertical consciousness gives way to a melodic-monodic one: a germ
of linearity. While Mahler's part-writing seldom bursts the harmonic framework, it nevertheless behaves, unlike that of Reger, for
example, as if it just tolerated the *basso continuo* scheme without
quite believing in it; Mahler's counterpoints jostle with insubordi-
nate joy against the harmonies. In the Sixth Symphony, counterpoint's inclination toward dissonance is allied to the major-minor
polarity. The counterpoints tend toward the mode opposite their
accompanying harmonies. This reappears in *Das Lied von der Erde*.
The post-Wagnerian idea of harmonic polyphony is perhaps under-
mined more by Mahler than even by *Salome* and *Elektra*, where
tonal and polyphonic forces play side-by-side without unduly im-
portuning each other, whereas Mahler's structure results largely
from the tension between them.

Because instrumentation is not covered by the traditional teaching
of composition, it is particularly suited in Mahler to interact both
with the individual strata of composition and with the totality. The
orchestra resisted Mahler's specific musical intentions less than did

form or harmony, for example. His effortless freedom in the use of instrumentation earned him early on, like Bruckner, a reputation for mastery—a reputation not entirely free of the insidious turn of mind that distinguishes categorically between the outer garment, the "window-dressing," of music and the inner substance. In Mahler's instrumentation, however, there can be as little question of window-dressing as of mastery of the kind the cliché has in mind. Instead of adapting to what the orchestra inflicts on it day by day, his ear devises countermeasures. They are no minor ingredient of his manner of instrumentation; the often bizarre registers of the Sixth Symphony, its frequently paradoxical combinations of forte and piano in different instruments and groups, create a sound that is as it is through preventing what would result from more conventional composition or directions. Nowhere is Mahler's music inspired primarily by a sense for sound. In this he was, initially, rather inept. The lack of expertise is remarkable in a conductor of his experience. At first he was seldom able to achieve the glowing orchestral tutti that even the most minor representatives of the New German school copied from Wagner, insofar as he ever aimed at it. The rounded, closed, voluminous sound is strikingly absent from the symphonies of his youth, and when Mahler needs it later it follows as if as a matter of course from the composition, without additional measures.

> Mahler's orchestra takes no part in the New German school's luxuriation in color. What is decisive in Mahler's instrumentation is the contour. Anything colorful is treated with almost contemptuous severity and disregard.[18]

But instrumentation in Mahler, which, by the criteria of Wagner or Schreker, appears dry or incorporeal, suits its purpose not through asceticism but as a true portrayal of the composition, and to that extent is decades ahead of its time. Here too virtue and necessity collaborate. With regard to the music's outward form, the demand for clarity converges with the nature of integral composition. Color becomes a function of the composition, which it discloses; the composition in turn is a function of the colors of which it is molded. Functional instrumentation, however, is productive for the sound itself, creating its Mahlerian life. The instrumentation is such that every principal part is unconditionally, unmistakably audible. The relation of essential and accidental is part of the acoustic phenomenon; nothing confuses the musical sense. Hence Mahler criticizes the ideal of euphony that encourages the sound to puff itself up around the music, to ruffle its feathers. Furthermore, Mahler's characters need that articulated diversity from which the whole arises, colors that are characteristic like the single melodic or harmonic events, not pleasing in themselves. Mahler's color, too, becomes characteristic at the expense of a harmonious, opulent sound free of sharp corners. These desiderata lead to a procedure of instrumentation at one with itself. The sound of *Das Lied von der Erde* and the Ninth Symphony is no less their character than their other musical properties.

Mahler's capacity for an instrumentation that characterizes is accompanied by a knowledge of the possibilities of the uncharacteristic that he acquired in extreme maturity. If in the 3/4 final section of *Das Lied von der Erde* he entrusts a low C major chord to three trombones in open position, the sound as such, despite its echoing sonority, does not attract attention, does not disturb the gradually vanishing whole. As important for great art in instrumentation as the ability to produce effects is the capacity to avoid or circumscribe them, to elaborate latency. The extreme contrast to this is represented by the solo trombones, in a sense cut loose, liberated from the assembly of the chorale, in the Third Symphony. Mahler was, indeed, the first to discover the trombone for its solo color. In the Third, or in a number of passages in the Funeral March and the Scherzo of the Fifth Symphony, it realizes what its name promises, what the ear hopes for in vain from a trombone section in several parts. To be sure, it is enabled to do so by the music, which is put into the mouth of the giant voice, those figures midway between recitative and theme, melos and fanfare, in which improvising chance and emphasis are interwoven. This is reinforced by the rhythm, the prose-like, over-long pauses.[19] It is only the disappearance of these in the continuation,[20] the melody becoming tauter, that unleashes the *wild* (wild) character that was gathering in the preceding *Wieder schwer* (heavy) episode. Such instrumentation was from the beginning nonconformist. The Finale of the First

Symphony contains a monstrous sound effect: bellowing trombone chords directly before the end of the first theme complex, at the point where its aimless storm explodes in momentary outbreaks.[21] The passage, which potentiates the trombones with trumpets and muted horns *fff*, resembles, with its pauses for air, the static cries of terror in the final dance of the victim of Stravinsky's *Sacre*. Hardly anywhere else does Mahler's music sound so undomesticated: the color dreams what was only fully composed a generation later. But even here the sound is summoned by the music, by the need for a concentration of something otherwise too chaotic, impetuous, and timeless, and more palpably by the dissonant clashing of the upper part in eighth notes against the supporting harmonies, which the dissonances of color reflect. Mahler wrote advanced timbres where they are least expected. In the midst of the self-affirming E-flat major of the Hymn in the Eighth Symphony, a field anticipates something of Webern's last works. The timbre of the "Infirma"[22] with the soloistic brass,[23] is that of Webern's cantatas, as if Mahler had wanted to submerge in this affirmative and retrospective work a secret message for the future. Hardly less astonishing is an instrumental moment in the Fourth Symphony, so innocent on the surface, at the transition from the first to the second theme of its variations and at the analogous points later. An imperceptible dying away is instrumentally extended.[24] A wind chord on the tonic, held for a whole note, leads diminuendo into a second, on the dominant; the winds, however, hold this for only a quarter note, while it is taken over simultaneously, on the first beat, in identical form by an almost imperceptible entry of violas divided into three sections, and harp harmonics; the color change is repeated. In it reverberate the thematic incidents that have already come to rest in the ritardando. In this inconspicuous passage one may well discern the model for the changing chords in Schoenberg's op. 16, the draft of the later *Klangfarbenmelodie*, the transformation of color into a constructive element in its own right. The idea probably has its origin in the overture to *Lohengrin*. Changes of timbre are effected in Mahler not only by means of chords but through individual notes, such as the sustained f' of the horns in the second trio of the Scherzo of the Fifth Symphony.[25] Egon Wellesz, in his essay in *Anbruch* published in

1930, instructively analyzed the instrumentation of this passage;[26] its resemblance to the color crescendo on the B before the night tavern scene in *Wozzeck* that has become famous, particularly to what Berg called the "inner life" of that note, is undeniable. However, constructive instrumentation is also to be observed on a large scale in Mahler. Bekker drew attention to the fact that the breakthrough, the vision of the brass in the second movement of the Fifth Symphony, only has its power because the brass had previously been silent. Similarly, the string Adagietto, in reality a self-contained introductory field to the Rondo Finale, which draws on it thematically, is formally influential through its contrast to the overall sound of the symphony, in which the winds were hitherto predominant. Sound patterns extending over long stretches bring about a plasticity of form; in this spirit Alban Berg separated smaller ensembles from the whole orchestra for certain scenes in *Wozzeck*, like the adagio in the street or the beginning of Act I, used a different orchestra for each of his *Frühe Lieder*, and finally, in *Lulu*, allocated their own orchestra groups to some of characters. In *Das Lied von der Erde* the instrumentation is varied slightly, as in Berg, for each piece. The trumpets are used extremely sparingly, tuba and timpani are brought in for only one piece; Mahler's ear may have felt that, unlike the accepted oriental percussion instruments, the timpani might have endangered the stylistic principle of exoticism, and in a symphony for solo parts the tuba's sound was probably too heavy. Despite the unified basic instrumental color of the whole cycle, the individual songs are differentiated through color from each other. The chamber-music sound of the *Kindertotenlieder* is admitted as an aspect of the large orchestra. In the very late Mahler, through the reintegration of a sound that had previously been dissected into its individual parts for the sake of clarity, the tutti is also compressed, dimmed, analogous to the "muted forte" occasionally demanded by Schoenberg. Mahler's art of instrumentation is a force field, not a style. The need for distinctness and characterization is opposed by that for integration, for a binding agent like that used to thicken soups. The configuration of the distinct and the bound might be studied in relation to Mahler's art of doubling, particularly of the woodwind. It clarifies the parts that it reinforces, but always has a

coloristic purpose as well. The combination of two colors produces a
third, strictly appropriate to the character of the theme, sometimes,
as in certain passages of the *Kindertotenlieder* and analogous ones in
"Der Einsame in Herbst," an organ-like difference tone. The unison
of the four flutes at the beginning of the development of the Fourth
is qualitatively different from the flute sound; the six clarinets in the
introductory melody of the first of Schoenberg's orchestral songs
op. 22 may even have their origin here. If the principle of a homogeneous sound leads on its own to poor filling-in parts, without it the
clearest instrumentation would remain abstract. Mahler is the great
exponent of instrumentation because he derived his procedure from
this contradiction, just as in the delineation of his works a vivid precision of detail and the vital flow of the whole are not in conflict, but
live on each other. His orchestra resists the illusory Wagnerian in-
finity, too sensuous for sober gray; nowhere in his work does prac-
ticality impair the richness of detail. But the orchestra throws off the
heavy folds of instrumentation as Mahler's harmony often does
those of the disguised four-part chorale, most consistently in the
Kindertotenlieder and some of the other Rückert songs, the archetypes of the chamber orchestra of the future. Mahler's music becomes incorporeal because it sounds as it specifically is. Even the
sound, the most sensual of all the dimensions of music, is made a
carrier of spirit.

7

Through spiritualization Mahler overthrew the criterion of immediacy and naturalness, an exponent of the same modernism that also made obsolete the sacrosanct notion of nature lyricism. Art's appearance of being the utterance of creation is shattered by the recognition of its own reified elements; respect is paid to suppressed nature only in that Mahler never supposes it as already there, that he never celebrates its surrogates. Only as something unattainable, debased in the wrongly socialized society, is its idea given outward appearance. Technically it leads to a dismantling of traditional language, before which Mahler still hesitated. Only because nothing in nature can be taken for granted, that it has consistently been as reduced as it appears virtually in Mahler's fragments, can it be autonomously constructed. For this reason Mahler's sounds often breach the closed acoustic space, leading their free life heedless of the sensuous unity of the total sound. No differently must music as a whole disintegrate into its elements for the sake of a unity that is no longer dictated to it. Like the trombone in the Third Symphony, since Schoenberg's Orchestral Pieces op. 16 all colors have spoken. Through the disregard of the single phenomenon for a priori systems of meaning, the music is trained to seek concrete ones. Precisely Mahler's sound has a peculiarly centrifugal quality. It strives away from the spherical acoustic form: through the frequent omission of horn pedal points, through the unsensuous use of strings in brittle, high positions, and later by chamber groupings or soloistic writing in the totality. Distinctness itself: the sound that honestly shows everything and no more than takes place in the composition is akin to disintegration. The more sharply the elements of composition are distinguished, the more remote they at first become to each other, the more resolutely they renounce a primary identity.

The idea of disintegration is announced oddly in the third movement of the First Symphony. In its sections in canon it is, in its simple way, more intricately woven than most of Mahler's earlier works. By parodying the cannon's dogmatic aspect, it negates it; that is why it allows remote colors like the solo double bass and the tuba that carries the melody to become prominent in a way that must have sounded scurrilous at the time. The disintegrating tendency then overtakes the movement in shock moments such as the sudden acceleration. At the same time the movement, the first in Mahler to do so, becomes static, superimposing strata on each other; its striking originality is produced by the unity of the disorganized and the significant. So early does the disintegrating tendency thus enter the procedure of composition. Its domain is form. For the sake of a novel-like flow, the form approximates to prose. The tonal Mahler knows the atonal means of linking through disconnectedness, the unmitigated contrast of "breaking out"[1] or breaking off[2] as a means of form. Sound as a simultaneous gestalt results from the individual sounds and their demands; Schoenberg expressly requires it for the performance of the third orchestral piece from op. 16. In the first movement of the Ninth the disintegrative tendency also takes possession of the manner of composing: incessant crossing and overlapping of its parts fray the lines; the composition too repudiates the strict distinction between the identical and nonidentical, the ordering principle of recent western music. Harmony collaborates in the disintegration, negating the fundamental idea as if under a spell. No more than the atonality that followed him does Mahler think in terms of centers of gravity. He clings to no musical first principle, his symphonies casting doubt on the postulate of a *prima musica*. The expression mark *schwebend* (floating) comments on more than the passages it characterizes; as compared to the awareness of scale degrees, Mahler's earlier marches and dances float no less than the emancipated last works. However, the tendency toward dissociation is, as a revolt against the assured center resting within itself, also one of content. What finally rejects the intrinsic connections of form is the broken image of the Other; integral form is this world.

Hence the greatest difficulty that Mahler presents to understanding. In flagrant contradiction to everything familiar from absolute, program-less music, his symphonies do not exist in a simple positive sense, as something granted to the participants as a reward: on the contrary, whole complexes want to be taken negatively—one should listen, as it were, against them. "We see an alternation of positive and negative situations."[3] A stratum that was reserved to literature and painting is conquered by absolute music. The brutally intrusive passage in the coda of the first movement of the mature Sixth Symphony[4] is heard directly as an irruption of the horrible. To conventional thinking this seems literary and unmusical; no music ought to be able to say no to itself. But Mahler's music is receptive precisely through its stringent capacity to do so, which extends into its selectively indiscriminate material, a content that is both non-conceptual and yet incapable of being misunderstood. Negativity for him has become a purely compositional category: through the banal that declares itself banal; through a lacrimose sentimentality that tears the mask from its own wretchedness; through a hyperbolical expression in excess of the music's actual meaning. Negative too—though without the transfiguring greatness of their models, the endings of the first movements of the Kreutzer Sonata and the Appassionata—are the catastrophes in the second movement of the Fifth, in the Finale of the Sixth, in the first movement of the Ninth. In them the composition passes judgment on its own activities. Before the might of this judgment the objection that all this is merely the subjective projection of the listener becomes the gesticulation of helpless competence. The negative elements are composed without room for optional perceptions. Often the purely musical characters are stamped exclusively by such intentions. In each the history of musical language is encapsulated. Nowhere has the material been beyond history; the mode of its arrival in the hands of the composer is inseparable from features of its likeness or unlikeness to what has been, the obsolete, the present. Every musical detail is more than it merely is by virtue of its place in musical language, of something historical. From this general circumstance Mahler derives his specific effect. The movement of the symphonic content in his work is that of the rising and falling, the colliding and mingling, of what the material has submerged within itself. He summons its often half-forgotten contents to a second life through technique. One who hears a Romantic piece from the past played by a meager, depleted orchestra with a piano in place of the harp rises up in protest not against the sound of the piano as such, which he is fond of elsewhere, but because the orchestra cannot purge the instrument of the sound to which the Salon orchestra has degraded it. Such strata, including their negativity, have been made fruitful by Mahler for composition itself. Because his material was obsolete, the new not yet set free, in Mahler the antiquated, what had fallen by the wayside, has become a cryptogram of the sounds as yet unheard that follow it. In the negativity of his music, its lack of outward immediacy, he has what is lacking in Bruckner, the trace of past suffering in his language.

How much Mahler's intrinsic musical negativity runs counter to the enthusiastic program of Berlioz or Liszt is shown by the fact that Mahlerian novels have no heroes and honor none, unlike those noisily proclaimed in two titles of Strauss and countless ones of Liszt. Even in the Finale of the Sixth, despite the hammer blows which, in any case, have not been properly heard hitherto and no doubt await their electronic realization, one will look in vain for the figure who is supposed to be smitten by fate. The music's abandonment to unbridled affect is its own death, the unabated vengeance of the world's course on Utopia. The dark and even despairing parts[5] recede in that movement behind others of turbid brooding, of overflowing exuberance, of rising tumult; the only real exceptions are the bilious wind chorale in the introduction and the trombone passage in the coda. The catastrophes coincide with the climaxes. It sometimes sounds as if at the moment of the final conflagration humanity grew incandescent again, the dead came to life once more. Joy flares high at the edge of horror. The first movement of *Das Lied von der Erde*, in the same key, and in keeping with the poetic theme, has compressed both into one and thus finally deciphered the major-minor transition. It is music itself that describes its parabolic path, not a human being designated by it, and certainly no individual. For this reason, in Mahler, the type of symphonic conflict of the *Eroica* is progressively invalidated. The development of the Second Symphony still complies with the pattern of a collison of hostile forces, a battle. The programmatic, intentional aspect of this is unmistakable, the process slightly unconvincing. From this Mahler's symphonies learn that the dramatic category of decision—usually avoided in any case by Beethoven, who ratifies something already accomplished rather than deciding it directly in his music— is alien to music. The weariness that, in the Second Symphony, follows the battle in the manner prescribed by musical handbooks, betrays in reality the chimerical nature of the effort to enact such things musically. The thesis of the thematic dualism in the sonata form was probably so inadequate from the first because it carried over the dramatic category of conflict into music unexamined. For music's temporal flow cannot entirely rid itself of an objective element, one of *temps espace*. Never, not even by symphonic contraction, does it pass so totally into the present moment as does the pure present of the subject, whose decision as an act of reason in a sense abolishes time. That is why the first movement of Mahler's Third brutally and with reason criticizes the dramatic logic of the Second. In Mahler music for the first time becomes aware of its radical divergence from tragedy.

This implies the answer to the most popular argument against Mahler, that he aimed for great effects but failed to achieve them. This is as much a part of the interior decoration of bourgeois taste and the bourgeois ideology of genuineness as the cliché that Karl Kraus was vain or had written himself out; it is bitterly to be regretted that Kraus, who kept aloof from great music, wrote no apology for Mahler, confining himself to a gloss on the Hoftheater directors who "were asleep on Gustav Mahler's death and learned of it in the morning from their obituaries."[6] Kraus too, incidentally, was judged by the facile criterion of naturalness and accused of contrivance and intellectualism. As in the case of the brokenness of Mahler's themes, which is measured against supposedly spontaneous inspiration, the automatic defense mechanism is guided here by the model of tragedy. The antipathies to Mahler sometimes reveal more precise experiences than the effusions at the stage exit. Much that, to those all too proficient in reality, cannot be involuntary enough in art is deliberately intended by Mahler, in keeping with Schoenberg's maxim that he who seeks nothing finds nothing. Often he formulates a figure because it is required at this particular moment. The mind that would abandon itself passively to the sensuous material must first obtain or prepare it, to be able to obey it. The objective temper needs subjective intervention to be realized. Nothing that passes into the epic totality remains unchanged. The specific, unschematic idea of each movement is the magnet of its episodes. Mahler does not evade the aporia that the unbound individual part can only be incorporated into a whole if it is preformed in keeping with the desiderata of that whole. He does not merely listen with devout attention for this themes, he sidles into them; it is often noticeable that they are there for the sake of their functions, such as that of extreme contrast; the lyrical theme of the first movement of the Sixth Symphony is the familiar example of such necessity. This necessity is incorrigible, arising from the objective problems of form. The whole is to crystallize from the individual impulses without regard to preconceived types. But these cannot be redeemed from their contingency. They can be synthesized only if they are already informed by the potential of the whole, and for this the composition must have discreet, invisible control: an element of deception cannot be excluded. Detail and totality, even uncompleted ones, do not merge seamlessly. Whatever their genesis might be, the stigmata of contrivance in Mahler testify to the impossibility of reconciling general and particular in a form exempt from the compulsion of a system. In them Mahler's music atones for turning away from the frame that no longer supports it, yet which still, and for long, lays claim to unanimous meaning. That Mahler, nevertheless, does not more adroitly conceal such objectively founded incompatibility benefits the content of his music. Where it sounds contrived, fruitlessness itself speaks from it, and nominalist art as such. In face of this, the over-hasty question as to what is intentional in Mahler's expression of overexertion and what is involuntary is as secondary as such concerns always are: in the art-work it is the form and its implications that count, not the subjective conditions of its genesis. To ask about the intention is to seek a criterion extraneous to the work and almost inaccessible to knowledge. Once the objective logic of the art-work has been set in motion, the individual producing it is reduced to a subordinate executive organ. However, Mahler could not be defended against incomprehension by denying the contrivance and stylizing him into a Schubert that he was not and did not wish to be.[7] Rather, that element would have to be deduced from the content. The truth of Mahler's music is not to be abstractly opposed to the elements in which it falls short of its intention. It is the truth of the unattainable. It is contrived both as a will to reach the unattainable, to go beyond the insufficiency of existence, and also as a sign of the unattainable itself. It says that human beings want to be redeemed and are not, which means untruthfulness or New German megalomania to those who themselves oppose its coming about.

The technical theater of contrivance and overexertion as an element in the content of truth in his work is Mahler's writing of melodies. The composer creates melodies where he intervenes, as it were, from outside, urges the process onwards, instead of simply letting the objective impulse take its course; at moments Beethoven proceeded likewise, as when his resolve breaks through in the last part of the development of large movements. This element is alien to the composition and inherent in it at the same time. Something of this resides in the capacity of marches to "sweep along" their listeners; they issue a command to the marchers even as they mimetically anticipate their steps. According to this pattern Mahler's music seeks to mobilize its listeners. What in Beethoven still appealed to pure feeling without consequences, the wish to "strike sparks from the soul," in Mahler resists pure contemplation. As if he had made Tolstoy's criticism of the Kreutzer Sonata his own, he wishes to advance to the practical stage. He beats his head against the wall of mere aesthetic image-making. While he, chained to the unconceptual and unobjective material of all music, can never say what the music upholds and what it opposes, he seems to say it nevertheless. This gives insight into the constellation of subjective and objective in his work. He is as often rebuked for high-flown subjectivity as his songs and symphonies, which are not content with the first person, are charged with objectivity. The contradiction could be resolved by noting that subjectivity motivates the movement of the whole toward its fulfillment, yet is not reproduced in the movement. The Mahlerian subject is less a soul that bears witness to itself than a political will unconscious of itself, which makes the aesthetic object a metaphor of that which it cannot induce real people to espouse. But since physical praxis is denied to art, which hankers after it, art cannot succeed in its enterprise, nor can Mahler divest himself of a residue of ideology. This then manifests itself in aesthetic acts of violence like his manner of writing melodies. But these actions also have their reason in the melodies themselves. At Mahler's time overtaxed tonality and popular melody both needed stimulants. Mahler had to have complete command of the derivative materials in order to set the petrified, dead matter in motion. The secondary, broken themes with which he operates no longer have the primary impulse that may once have given them a life of their own. But Mahler intends to go further, not to acquiesce. Such conflict becomes a factor in the composition. Because an identity between the subjective driving force and the objective law of motion is not attained, the lines are extended beyond what they and their implied harmonies can yield by nature. In Mahler's time melody was altogether problematic. The tonal possibilities of combination, particularly the diatonic ones, are too stale to allow that novelty that, since the beginnings of Romanticism, was the criterion of melody. The new, chromatic configurations tend, at least at the beginning of the Wagnerian and post-Wagnerian phase, toward diminution, reduction to the short motive, in keeping with the small melodic steps; only in the New Music did large, free melodies arise, where they were intended, from emancipated chromaticism. Strauss once admitted that only short, fragmentary motives really had occurred to him; in Reger melody is atomized into semitone steps devoid of quality, which cement one harmony to another. The Straussian-Berliozian technique of the *imprévu*, of interruption as effect, of permanent surprise, seeks to make a virtue of this necessity by turning it into a *principium stilisationis*. Mahler drew the inverse conclusion, commanding melody against its wishes and so giving the melodies themselves their cachet, in a way remotely analogous to Beethoven's device of damming up the tonal flow by the disposition of the *sforzati* and leaving behind in it, as it were, a trace of subjectivity. *Wie gepeitscht* (as if whipped onwards), the Scherzo of Mahler's Sixth Symphony is marked in one place. Since the long melody from the Finale of his First he has no more spared his themes than a coachman obsessed by his destination does his collapsing horses. But what he inflicts on the music carries it forwards, as an urging beyond the intrinsic measure, an exertion to the breaking point, a transcendence of yearning. In many cases in Mahler the motives already describe within themselves, in the smallest compass, transcendent movements, and accentuate them harmonically through illusory progressions, as the so-called spear motive did in *Parsifal*, where it appears in the modulating D major sections of the prelude first in the violas and the "alto oboe"—the English horn— then is taken up by the oboes and cellos, and then, returning to A-flat major, arrives fortissimo with the violins and diverse woodwinds, still deceptively modulating, in the foreground.[8] In a similar way Mahler often reaches up to a quarter note with three eighth notes ascending in seconds; the melody then falls by a second to a stressed dotted quarter note. The strong beat is then heard, whether immediately or on being repeated, over other harmonies than those expected. Such passages offer the paradox of a prepared surprise that recurs as an artifice in Berg. The Other, the unexpected, is glimpsed already in that which is transcended. Such moments are insatiable. They must especially confuse those who listen to Mahler with demands drawn from outside. Again and again the attempt is made, as if the repulsed music hoped at last to break through: "Ach nein, ich ließ mich nicht abweisen." (No, I would not be turned away.) Insatiably the melodies are created, insatiable sometimes is the tone of the single figures, and the formal structure. The content, which cannot endure the narrow bounds, the justification of the finite, makes the musical language obey it, sabotages the aesthetic norm of moderation and order. That is the damage that unattained transcendence leaves behind in the coherence of the immanent. The affect collides with civilization, which silences it as something uncouth; insatiable music is the result of the conflict. It violates the mimetic taboo.[9] He who cannot contain himself flees to unconceptual language, which still allows unbounded weeping and unbounded love. At times that flight is accompanied in the music's form by a peculiar sense of the coming after: what yearns to go beyond itself is at the same time a leave-taking, a remembrance. The word *entlächelnd* in an early poem by Werfel gives the same impression of a departing smile. Such a feeling inhabits the motive type of the first violins in the consequent phrase marked *mit Empfindung* (with feeling) of the Adagietto of the Fifth.[10] The idea of transcendence has become the graphic curve of music. Mahler's manner of writing melodies is by no means explained by a lack of what is vulgarly called inspiration— Mahler himself, incidentally, did not question that category. When he was of a mind to, he produced as many original melodic ideas as he wished; examples could be easily assembled from the Andante of the Second Symphony up to the unparalleled main theme of the Adagio of the Tenth. Rather, the heretical manipulation of melodies follows from Mahler's latent structural law, what Riegl too psychologically calls his "artistic volition." Violence is done to the melodies for the sake of the whole, which Mahler's memory, for all his obsession with detail, never for a moment let out of sight.

The charge of contrivance in Mahler is regularly associated with that of his being bound by his time. The one who allegedly wanted to do more than he was able is seen as the hollow, puffed-up subject of late liberalism, Romanticism's period of decay. No matter how few bridges lead to Strauss, to whom they owe the idea of their existence: pure chronology encourages a comparison between him and Mahler. About the time of *Salome* the choice between them, Alban Berg tells us, was extremely difficult. Strauss's light hand not only scattered his illustrative effects across a fabric both assured and surprising: the linking of associations made his structure both more mobile and, in his best pieces, better articulated. Strauss, on the surface so much the modern Impressionist, was more at home in the intricate traditional manipulation of motives than was Mahler; for just that reason the process of disintegration advanced further in him than did Mahler's technique, which, for all its irregularity, was at first rather straightforward. In face of Strauss's manner of con-

quering time by incessantly engaging and intriguing the ear,
Mahler's seems trustingly anachronistic. The young Mahler
allowed himself to be guided by something floating more or less
vaguely before him, rather than composing according to a presiding
will; hence his pieces, in comparison with those of a Strauss controlled in every note, injecting life into the remotest voices, ap-
peared clumsy. But Strauss controls his materials with such
nonchalant assurance just because he is little concerned where the
music is seeking to go by its own inner logic. He treats it as a continuum of connected effects, each calculated in relation to the others. They are organized down to the smallest detail, but they are, as
it were, imposed on the music, locked together with it according to a
fixed scheme. The need to discern patiently and to reconstruct musically the purely objective tendencies of the themes and of the whole
is ignored. Measured by a more exacting concept of technique, the
far more expert Strauss is technically inferior to Mahler, because
the latter's structure is objectively more binding. Mahler's metaphysical intention is realized in that he is drawn along by the objective forces inherent in his work as if he were his own detached
spectator. If the style of his music, by virtue of the unity of his epoch, cannot historically escape the concept of "Life," which also includes Debussy's irrational nuances and Strauss's brio, its content is
less the affirmative echo of vitalism than is the case with them.
Rather, he resembles the metaphysical philosophies that reflected
the idea of life, Bergson and the late Simmel. Simmel's formula of
life as more than life does not sit ill on Mahler. The difference between Strauss's high-bourgeois, vitalistic musical gratification and
the transcendent concerns of Mahler is not, however, merely one of
what is expressed, but of what in musical terms is composed. In
Mahler the form forgets itself. In Strauss it remains the mise-en-
scène of a subjective consciousness that never breaks free of itself,
which, for all its concentration on externals, never externalizes itself
in the musical object. Strauss never advanced beyond the immediacy of talent and, ossifying within it, was obliged to copy himself,
to write *Joseph-Legende* and the Alpine Symphony, not to mention
desolate late works like *Capriccio*. What is gropingly initiated in
Mahler did not fall prey to the smart jargon of the Wilhelmine era.

It led him to the mastery of being so and not otherwise, while Strauss ended in concordance with commodity film music, which took its revenge on his false naïveté, his collusion. The very late Beethoven, the archetype of the grandiose late style, was a precursor as was Mahler. His historical position is that of latent modernism, as was Van Gogh's, who still felt himself to be an Impressionist and was the opposite. The early Mahler, despite a basic standpoint that was conservative in principle, has something in common with the Fauvist aspects of the beginnings of the new painting. The resistance to movements like the deliberately discontinuous slow movement of the First Symphony on the part of the proprietors of culture, the self-inflicted conviction that such work could not be taken seriously, is accompanied by the knowledge that there was some truth in it after all, and that it was perhaps precisely the part giving offense that contained the truth that really mattered. The scoffing at such movements and passages in Mahler is always, at the same time, a solidarity with them; the listener defects to him. Seldom does the abrupt appearance of novelty harmonize with a perfect mastery of the collapsing tradition. If Mahler's music at first assorts ill with the concept of quality, it reminds that concept of the wrong done to it, of its naïvely immaculate, obdurate persistence in a closed circle of technique and taste, which conjures before the music a deceptive façade of validity. The violation of such standards by Mahler, whether intentional or not, becomes objectively a means of artistic expression. If his gestures are infantile, he spurns being adult because his music has seen to the bottom of adult culture and wants to be no part of it. It would be easy to demonstrate time-bound tendencies in precisely those composers of the past whom Mahler's judges believe to be a capital eternally secure: routine mistakes in Bach and Mozart, the admixture of decorative Empire heroism in Beethoven, of the oleograph in Schumann, of the salon in Chopin and Debussy. It is only as such aspects of significant music wither away that a content is revealed that would itself have been stunted without the nourishment found in such strata. The distinction between time-bound and lasting qualities is invalid because what lasts, in music as well, is nothing other than "its time grasped in ideas."[11] In the end the idea of lastingness itself reifies the life of works as a fixed possession, instead of conceiving it as an unfolding and dying away that befits all human formations. Mahler's symphonies have been compared to Romanesque railroad stations and to cathedral-like department stores.[12] But his formal imagination would never have emancipated itself without the aspiration to the monumental. Had he been content with intimate genre formats, the musically decisive question as to the construction of duration would not have been posed. The prospect of the grandiose, no matter how unsteady, that his era opened before him was the background of his metaphysical élan, high above the mediocre norm of the same age. How little the wretched concept of a time-bound element that has to be subtracted as a residue from the lasting and eternal does justice to his or any significant work; how much, rather, its truth-content is immersed in a temporality most deftly criticized by those whose superiority to what they dishonor by honoring it resides solely in having been born later—this is seen in what monumentality became in Mahler. He set out to write exalted songs, and wrote *Das Lied von der Erde*. The fact that affirmation foundered again and again in his development is his triumph, the only one without shame, the permanent defeat. He refuted monumental decor by seeing his immoderate exertion refuted by the monumental entity to which it was addressed. He does not fail merely by failing. The authenticity of his last works, which turn their backs on all fictions of salvation, could have been attained by no lesser risk. The Finale of the Sixth Symphony has its pre-eminence in Mahler's oeuvre because, more monumentally composed than all the rest, it shatters the spell of affirmative illusion. The present-day allergy to the colossal is not absolute: it too has its tribute to pay. For it the conception of art as the manifestation of the idea that would be the whole dissolves into nothing. Quality is not so indifferent to quantity as it has come to appear now that the latter has become sour grapes. They cannot be picked any more, but perhaps saved by reflection. The heartbreaking power of breaking-through would not have been accorded to Mahler had there not glowed to white heat in him that which the devotees of a musical baroque, which, incidentally, does not exist, arraign as Romantic subjectivism. Mahler, filled with the tension of what, from the standpoint of the philosophy of history, was at the same time overdue and impossible, survives solely on the strength of what is temporal in him. More open to criticism is the fact that the reality other than the world's course, the moment of transcendence, the suspension of the immanent structure and its formal categories, itself hardens to a category, a fixed component of form. Anyone who knows the language of his symphonies foresees not without apprehension: now the structure is to be loosened, breached, now the episode will unfailingly broaden out. For this reason too, not merely in the course of musical logic, Mahler's military calls and natural sounds are petrified. His music is threatened by what it would least want to be, ritual. Its presence is felt even in disproportions of form, in overextensions of even the most magnificent episodes, like the Burlesque in the Ninth Symphony with the accumulated glissandi. What is consoling in this are the inexhaustible riches Mahler has wrung from the fatal identity of that which signifies its opposite.

Only an apologist nervous to the point of obduracy could dispute that there are weak pieces by Mahler. Just as his forms never remain within the confines of the given, but everywhere make their own possibility and musical form itself their theme, each of them enters the zone of potential miscarriage. Aesthetic quality itself is not immune to his fractures. The work through which, probably, most have come to love Mahler, the Second Symphony, is likely to fade first, through loquacity in the first movement and the Scherzo, through some crudity in the "resurrection" Finale. The latter would have needed the thoroughgoing polyphony which the first movement of the Eighth takes upon itself; the long instrumental section garrulously divulges too much of the vocal section and seems loosely articulated, even the cries causing scarcely a shiver; only the *pp* entry of the choir and its theme retain suggestive power. The Adagietto of the Fifth, despite its important conception as an individual piece within the whole, borders on genre prettiness through its ingratiating sound; the Finale, fresh in many details and with novel formal ideas like that of the musical quick-motion picture, is undoubtedly too lightweight in relation to the first three movements. If opinions may differ over this, the Finale of the Seventh embarrasses even those who concede everything to Mahler. In a let-ter Schoenberg chose examples of Mahler's power of invention from precisely this movement.[13] But even they are peculiarly arrested in their growth. Even on the most strenuous immersion in the work, one will scarcely be able to deny an impotent disproportion between the splendid exterior and the meager content of the whole. Technically the fault lies with the steadfast use of diatonicism, the monotony of which was scarcely to be prevented, in view of such ample dimensions. The movement is theatrical: only the stage sky over the too-adjacent fairground meadow is as blue as this. The positivity of the *per aspera ad astra* movement in the Fifth, which surpasses even this Finale, can manifest itself only as a tableau, a scene of motley bustle; perhaps the Finale of Schubert's Great C Major Symphony, the last abundant work of symphonic positivity to be written, already tends secretly toward operatic performance. The limpid soaring of the solo violin in the first measure of the fourth movement of Mahler's Seventh, solace that follows like a rhyme the mourning of the tenebrous Scherzo, commands more belief than all the pomp of the Finale. Mahler in one place gently mocks it with the epithet *etwas prachtvoll* (rather ceremoniously), yet without the humor breaking through. The claim that the goal has been reached, the fear of aberrations *après fortune faite*, are answered depressingly by endless repetitions, particularly of the minuet-like theme. The tone of strained gaiety no more actualizes joy than the word *gaudeamus;* the thematic fulfillments announced too eagerly by the gestures of fulfilling do not materialize. Mahler was a poor yea-sayer. His voice cracks, like Nietzsche's, when he proclaims values, speaks from mere conviction, when he himself puts into practice the abhorrent notion of overcoming on which the thematic analyses capitalize, and makes music as if joy were already in the world. His vainly jubilant movements unmask jubilation, his subjective incapacity for the happy end denounces itself. In traditional forms it was still an inbuilt element and might slip through, provided convention relieved it of specific responsibility; it founders where the joke becomes serious. The affirmative movements may not, in the interests of balance, fall short of the first ones, if they are to appear as the result of a process. Bekker called works of this type finale-symphonies. They refuse the last dance, the less binding residue of the suite. But at the

same time they cannot deliver what they postulate. They are supposed to present solutions, obstacles overcome, and are not allowed
to repeat, still less to surpass the preceding tensions. The hackneyed
happy endings of earlier symphonies, like the wedding at the end of
comedies, took account of such limitations. Symphonic dynamics
no longer tolerate it, if the unity of movements, problematic in any
case, is not to be nullified. Because both alternatives are objectively
wrong, the problem of the finale, which Mahler was the first to
tackle radically, is at the same moment no longer soluble. His successful final movements are those that ignore the radiant path *ad
astra*. That of the Sixth Symphony heightens its first movement
and negates it; *Das Lied von der Erde* and the Ninth Symphony cir-
cumvent the difficulty with sublime instinct by no more feigning
homeostasis than they enact a positive outcome free of conflict, but
by looking questioningly into uncertainty. The end here is that no
end is any longer possible, that music cannot be hypostatized as a
unity of actually present meaning.

Such hypostasis is pursued by the official magnum opus,
the Eighth Symphony. The words "official" and "magnum opus"
(*Hauptwerk*) indicate the vulnerable points, the genre chef d'oeuvre,
Puvis de Chavannes, the ostentatious cardboard, the giant symbolic
shell. The magnum opus is the aborted, objectively impossible re-
suscitation of the cultic. It claims not only to be a totality in itself,
but to create one in its sphere of influence. The dogmatic content
from which it borrows its authority is neutralized in it to a cultural
commodity. In reality it worships itself. The spirit that names the
Hymn in the Eighth as such has degenerated to tautology, to a mere
duplication of itself, while the gesture of sursum corda underlines
the claim to be more. What Durkheim imputed to religions at about
the time the solemn festival performances from *Parsifal* to the
Eighth Symphony were coming into being, that they were self-
representations of the collective spirit, applies exactly to at least the
ritual art-works of late capitalism. Their Holy of Holies is empty.
Hans Pfitzner's jibe about the first movement, *Veni Creator Spiritus*: "But supposing He does not come," touches with the percipi-
ence of rancor on something valid. It is not as if Mahler lacked the
necessary strength—precisely the first theme is admirably apt for

those words—there is an element of genius in the idea of animating with trombones what Riemann calls a dead interval spanning the seventh between the first two elements of the motive, in the immediate continuation. But the invocation is addressed, according to an objective sense of form, to the music itself. That the Spirit should come is a plea that the composition should be inspired. By mistaking the consecrated wafer of the Spirit for itself, it confuses art and religion, under the sway of a false consciousness that extends from *Die Meistersinger* to Pfitzner's *Palestrina*, and to which the philosophical conceptions of Schoenberg, the man with *Die glückliche Hand*, the chosen one of *Die Jakobsleiter*, are also subject. Like no other composer of his time, Mahler was sensitive to collective shocks. The temptation that arose from this, to glorify the collective that he felt sounding through him as an absolute, was almost overwhelming. That he did not resist it is his offense. In the Eighth he repudiated his own idea of the radical secularization of metaphysical words, uttering them himself. If on this one occasion one were to speak of Mahler in the language of psychology, the Eighth, like the Finale of the Seventh, was an identification with the attacker. It takes refuge in the power and glory of what it dreads; its official posture is fear deformed as affirmation.

Both the social structure and the state of the aesthetic constituents of form prohibit the magnum opus. This is why the New Music has turned its back on the symphony; Schoenberg was unable to complete it, the potential of which was so manifest in *Die glückliche Hand*, or the oratorio and the Old Testament opera. The historical-philosophical preconditions were hardly more favorable for Mahler, and yet, naïve in this, he dared to write symphonies. He thus paid his tribute to the New Germanism, for which since Liszt nothing was too high or too dear as a subject for music, and which played its part in squandering the cultural heritage by producing secondary facsimiles of it. The Eighth is infected by the illusion that sublime subjects, the hymn *Veni Creator Spiritus*, the closing scene of *Faust*, guaranteed the sublimity of the content. But sublime subjects, to which the art-work attaches itself, are no more than its theme. That the content can be better preserved by negation than by demonstration is attested in exemplary fashion by Mahler's own music, in opposition to his consciousness. In the Eighth, however, he bowed to that vulgarization of the Hegelian aesthetic of content that flourishes today in Eastern parts. From the first organ chord on it is inspirited by the elevating enthusiasms of the festivals of song, reviving *Meistersinger* tones.[14] Simplification for the sake of exultation does not benefit the composition, despite masterful economy. The compressed polyphony of the first movement, which, as compared with the Second, has all the experience of the middle instrumental symphonies on its side, is stylizingly contained in a constricting *basso continuo* schema. Certainly, the dignity of the magnum opus in some places breaches its concept and thereby realizes it: perhaps this can only be measured by someone who still has the "Accende" in Anton von Webern's Vienna performance in his ears. There even the entry of the recapitulation retained its force. If all musical performance must come to the aid of the insufficiency of works, the Eighth needs the most perfect of all. The retrospectively closed sonata form of its first movement is adequately explained neither by the need for a contrast to the second nor by that for an intensification. Rather, sonata form allows something resembling a dialectic to the unflagging affirmation that is unconvincing even to itself. In the development the abyss of the wicked and fallible yawns even in musical terms, protecting the Hymn from the insipidly edifying. The *Faust* music, on the other hand, allows itself to be seduced by the phantasm of a great simplicity. If it borrows the theme to the words "Neige, neige" from a children's piece by Schumann, it is not overawed by the greatness of the words. It is striking how little it reproduces of what the poetry seems primarily to offer composition, the ascent from the mountain gorges to the heaven of Doctor Marianus. Rather, Mahler's epic contemplation derived from it a phenomenology of love. For this reason the music lacks the antithetical element of the Second Part, despite the lines on the painful earthly residue.

The only humanly interesting question is what was nevertheless successful in the magnum opus. This, however, is not merely the antithesis of the affirmative element; sheep and goats should not be separated even by one on the side of the goats. The affirmative intention of the Eighth is also Mahler's old concern with the break-through, and it does not entirely conform to the symphony's official aspect. When in the *Faust* music the boys' choir sings "Jauchzet laut, es ist gelungen," a shiver passes for a second through the lis-tener as if success were really achieved. Illusory yea-saying and a present free of illusions intertwine: only in terms of illusion is Mahler's primary impulse, that of the First Symphony, able once again to make itself heard in undomesticated form. The beneficiary of this, particularly in the second part, is the musical procedure. The choice of text, through the cantata-like architecture of the scene, with its lack of a recapitulation, suggested to Mahler the unfettered formal structure that became that of the late works. This very ex-tensive piece, executed in broad complexes, is no longer in sonata form, but neither is it a mere sequence of contrasting solo songs and choruses; endowed with a mighty, evolving subterranean flow, it is a "symphony" as was *Das Lied von der Erde*, with which it is strangely convergent. The experience of the sacrificed sonata form is not lost. The introduction expanded into the Adagio leads on dis-tinctly to a first theme in a full allegro tempo.[15] A number of the alla breve songs are the equivalent of a scherzo;[16] the fulfillment field of the pervading dynamic is the hymn of Doctor Marianus, "Blicket auf." The Chorus mysticus turns as if backwards, with the gesture of a coda. The movement's signature is the combination of inten-tionally simple basic harmonic relationships with voices diverging from them. The thoroughly inspired E-flat minor introduction brings the Mahlerian type of harmony, which leaves the earth be-hind it by imperceptible gradations, back to itself. Its potential en-ergy is actualized in the wild, fervent songs of the Pater ecstaticus and the Pater profundus. Enigmatically enough, Mahler gave the text something of the color of the cabbalistic Gevura.[17] That throughout the piece he mutes the gigantic orchestra to an accompa-niment furthers the disintegration of the sound by a certain caustic sharpness, and by soloistic mixtures; the second part of this work, notorious for its mass forces, is poor in cumulative mass effects; there can be no question in it of an excess of external means. The reason for the orchestra's size is probably Mahler's wish, for the sake of monumental effects, sometimes to use instrumentation to endow sounds made up of many different notes with a homogeneous color. All is poised on a knife-edge, uncurtailed Utopia and the lapse into grandiose decorativeness. Mahler's danger is that of the redeemer.

8

Mahler's music holds fast to Utopia in the memory traces from childhood, which appear as if it were only for their sake that it would be worth living. But no less authentic for him is the consciousness that this happiness is lost, and only in being lost becomes the happiness it itself never was. By a process of reversal the last works do justice to this conviction. They do not allow themselves to be deluded by the might and splendor to which the immanent musical context of the Eighth acquiesced, but seek to free themselves from the falsehood in it. It is not merely through the tone of leave-taking and death that Mahler leaves behind the affirmative excesses. The musical procedure itself no longer complies, bearing witness to a historical consciousness that inclines entirely without hope toward the living. The extreme states of the soul expressed in the late phase with means that, for the years after 1900, are still fairly traditional, alienate these means totally: the general is so saturated with the particular that it is only through the particular that it can recover a compelling generality. The girl in *Das Lied von der Erde* throws her secret lover "long yearning looks." Such is the look of the work itself, absorbing, doubting, turned backwards with precipitous tenderness, as previously was only the ritardando in the Fourth Symphony, but also like the gaze of Proust's *Recherche*, which came into being at about the same time; the unity of the years throws an unsteady bridge between two artists who knew nothing of each other and would scarcely have understood each other. The *jeunes filles en fleurs* of Balbec are the Chinese girls in Mahler who pick flowers. The end of "Von der Schönheit," the clarinet entry in the epilogue,[1] a passage the like of which is granted to music only every hundred years, rediscovers time as irrecoverable. In both, unfettered joy and unfettered melancholy perform their charade; in the prohibition of images of hope, hope has its last dwelling-place. This place is in both, however, the strength to name the forgotten that is concealed in the stuff of experience. Like Proust, Mahler rescued his idea from childhood. That his idiosyncratically unmistakable, unexchangeable aspect nevertheless became the universal, the secret of all, he has in advance of all of the music of his time; in this he was probably equaled among composers only by Schubert.

The child who thinks it is composing when it fumbles about on the keyboard ascribes endless relevance to each chord, each dissonance, each surprising turn. It hears them with the freshness of the first time, as if these sounds, though usually hackneyed, had never existed before, as if they were in themselves laden with everything it imagines while hearing them. This belief cannot be preserved, and those who seek to reinstate such freshness fall victim to the illusion that it already was.[2] Mahler, however, never allowed himself to be dissuaded of it and therefore tried to wrest it from deception. His movements, as wholes, would like to endow their musical content with the for-the-first-time quality that evaporates from each individual element, the endowing having the force of command, just as in Austrian dialect the word *anschaffen* (to get) also has the meaning "to command." All willfulness in the mastery of material he puts at the service of the involuntary. His symphonies became capable of this through ageing, their gradual saturation with experience, the medium of the epic art-work. This is shown early on by isolated passages, the more difficult to miss since they stand out from their surroundings by this specific quality. In the song "Liebst du um Schönheit," at the end of the cycle of the so-called "Last Seven," roughly contemporaneous with the Fifth Symphony, the singing voice closes on an A, the submediant, forming a discord with the tonic triad, as if the feeling found no outlet but suffocated in its excess. What is expressed is so overwhelming as to render the phenomenon, the language of music itself, indifferent. It does not finish its utterance; expression becomes a sobbing. What befalls it in such details takes hold of it entirely in the last pieces. Experience tinges all of the words and configurations of the music of the late Mahler, far beyond its functional importance, as it does otherwise only in the late style of great writers. The originality of *Das Lied von der Erde* has little to do with the traditional meaning of the term. Familiar phrases carried by the gradient of musical language are lit up: someone who says something familiar, but behind which his whole life stands, says something more and other than what he says. Music becomes a blotting paper, an everyday thing that becomes saturated with significance, allows it to appear without being subject to it. This redeployment of the trivial as of the abstract through experience was always Mahler's concern; in the late style it no longer admits the thought of triviality. Formulas from the last movement like "O sieh! wie eine Silberbarke schwebt der Mond"[3] or the parallel "Du, mein Freund, mir war in dieser Welt das Glück nicht hold,"[4] commonplace and unique in one, were previously found only in Beethoven's last works, or at most in Verdi's *Otello*, when the essence of whole ariose developments is stored up in a single motive: the making essential of the inessential through miniaturization, as in the little box of Goethe's *Neue Melusine*. The generality of a life and the almost material concretion of the moment are forced to stand still, the broken sensuous joy to attain the supra-sensuous. Relevant in this way is the almost vanishingly insignificant feature at the very beginning of the Ninth Symphony. There, in the serene D major, an accompanying voice of cellos and horns brings a B-flat into the cadence.[5] The minor pole of the old polarity is represented by a single note. As if by the application of acid, grief has drawn together in it, as if it were no longer expressed at all, but precipitated in the language. No differently, for the mature artist, is suffering the tacit precondition of everything he says. Music is a twitching at the corners of the mouth. In itself, in isolation, the flattered sixth would be banal, too naïve for what is meant. But it is healed, like the conventional element in general that is also tolerated by the late Mahler, by the density of the experience of fragility: the alienated musical means submit without resistance to what they proclaim. In this Mahler tends toward the documentary as Proust's novel does toward autobiography; this results finally from the will of art to transcend itself. The structure of meanings that assimilates every element coexists with disintegration, with the loosening of the aesthetic spell by material communicated without illusion.

In order, in Goethe's phrase, to "step back from appearances" and at the same time to imbue his music with the painful aroma of memory, the late Mahler inclines toward the exoticism of the period. China becomes a principle of stylization. In the arts-and-crafts texts by Hans Bethge used in *Das Lied von der Erde*, which in themselves were hardly assured of immortality, those elements were ignited in Mahler that may have been waiting for him in the old originals. The Ninth, however, of which it has rightly been said that it begins where *Das Lied von der Erde* ends, remains in the same theater. It continues to use the whole-tone scale in its melodic construction, and with consequence for the harmony, above all in the second and third movements. Mahler worked with the pentatonic scale and Far Eastern sounds at a time when, in the general movement of European art, all that was slightly outmoded, the whole-tone scale obsolete; he reconquers for the latter something of the shock that it had lost under Debussy's cultivation: where a whole-tone chord accompanies the "morschen Tand" of *Das Trinklied vom Jammer der Erde*,[6] the music seems to crumble away. Such elements are hardly to be enjoyed impressionistically any longer. Moreover, in Debussy as well, and the Strauss of *Salome*, exoticism was bound up with the evolution of the material; what was imported from outside into Western tonality shook the basis of its predominance, particularly as regards the cadence. In the late Mahler this musical inflection was to help entirely individualized effects to be attained with coinages already current. The inauthentic Chinese element, sketched with extreme discretion, plays a similar part to that of the folk song earlier: a pseudomorph that does not take itself literally but grows eloquent through inauthenticity. But by replacing the Austrian folk song by the remote, an Orient approved as a stylistic means, he divests himself of the hope of collective cover for what is his own. In this respect, too, the late works embody a Romanticism of disillusionment as do no others since Schubert's *Winterreise*. Mahler's exoticism was a prelude to emigration. In reality, after resigning as Director of the Vienna Opera, Mahler went to America; there he collapsed. Berg, too, played in the twenties with the idea of emigrating, replying to the question how he intended to come to terms with technical civilization by saying that over there it was at least consistently applied and it worked. Mahler's attitude to technical means was not dissimilar. *Das Lied von der Erde* has colonized a white area of the intellectual atlas, where a porcelain China and the artificially red cliffs of the Dolomites border on each other under a mineral sky. This Orient is pseudomorphous also as a cover for Mahler's Jewish element. One can no more put one's finger on this element than in any other work of art: it shrinks from identification yet to the whole remains indispensable. The attempt to deny it in order to reclaim Mahler for a conception of German music infected by National Socialism is as aberrant as his appropriation as a Jewish nationalist composer. Possibly synagogal or secular Jewish melodies are rare; a passage in the Scherzo of the Fourth Symphony[7] might most readily point in that direction. What is Jewish in Mahler does not participate directly in the folk element, but speaks through all its mediations as an intellectual voice, something non-sensuous yet perceptible in the totality. This, admittedly, abolishes the distinction between the recognition of this aspect of Mahler and the philosophical interpretation of music in general. The former is confined to the directly musical qualities and their technical organization, while the latter must take account of the spirit of the music. This can no more be grasped abstractly, by magic, than through unreflective, sensuous features. To understand music is nothing other than to trace the interaction of the two: to be musical converges with the philosophy of music. What, in the late style, no longer emanates from the manner of composition but from the material itself, the shrill, sometimes nasal, gesticulating, uproarious aspect, makes its own affair, and without extenuation, exactly the same quality of Jewishness that provokes sadism. The alienation effects in *Das Lied von der Erde* are faithfully imitated from the irritation that Far Eastern music unalterably causes the Western ear. The notion of the Chinese Wall is found in Karl Kraus and in Kafka. The story of the tam-tam stroke of the fireman in America might be taken from Kafka; it is supposed to have given Mahler a traumatic shock and probably recurs at the end of the "Purgatorio" fragment from the Tenth Symphony; in Mahler it was entirely possible for a firemen's band to play at the Last Judgment. His Utopia is worn out like the Nature Theater of Oklahoma. The ground trembles under the feet of the assimilated Jew—as of the Zionist; by the euphemism of foreignness the outsider seeks to appease the shadow of terror. That, and not merely the expression of a sick man's premonition of individual death, endows the last works with their documentary seriousness. Directly, with tangible connections through motives, the world of Chinese imagery of *Das Lied von der Erde* is derived from the biblical Palestine of the Faust music, particularly in the outwardly most cheerful song, "Von der Jugend." The exoticism is not content with the pentatonic and the whole-tone scales, but molds the whole texture; Mahler's old bass-lessness has its homecoming in the alien world. That which cannot be entirely reproduced in the remote musical system becomes an ingredient of meaning, as if the world of his past life had become as removed from the subject as such languages. Contributing not least to this is the high register of a tenor voice extensively denatured in the Chinese manner, which up to now has made performance prohibitively difficult: that and not the fear of his own work may have induced Mahler to cease producing it. The blurred unison in which identical voices diverge slightly through rhythm—since the *Kindertotenlieder* an improvised corrective to the all too pure art-song—is used with utmost logic. It also occurs in the Eighth, probably from the feeling of a divergence in the material between vocal and instrumental invention. But it is above all in *Das Lied von der Erde* that exoticism provides the thematic principle of construction. Mahler selects the critical tones from the pentatonic scale, the melodic sequence of second and third, that is, a deviation from the scale in seconds. It forms a latent primal motive. Wagner proceeded analogously, impelled by the exigencies of panchromaticism, in *Tristan*. This A–G–E motive in its uncounted modifications and transpositions—including inversion, retrograde, and rotation— is a formation midway between a thematic component and a piece of musical vocabulary, in which it is probably the last and most impressive model for the "basic shapes" (*Grundgestalten*) of Schoenberg's twelve-tone technique. As in the latter, the motive is also simultaneously folded together, as in the unresolved final chord of the work.

Das Lied von der Erde is a sequence of six orchestral songs, the last of considerable dimensions. In all, and particularly in the first piece, symphonic expansion bursts the limits of the song. Nevertheless, most of them, like Mahler's songs previously, are conceived in an unmistakably strophic manner. But the variants are extraordinarily far-reaching. They also extend into the tonal plan. Frequently the repeats of stanzas are on a different tonal level, only the end reverting to the original one; the perspectivist layering of harmonic regions from the symphonies is combined with strophic articulation. Only occasionally, as in "Von der Jugend" and "Der Trunkene im Frühling," are the ends and beginnings of stanzas evident as such; they are apt to be hidden by reassembly of the motivic material. In the outer movements the types of the development and the suspension field are merged into orchestral interludes before the reprise-like final stanzas; yet even the form of *Das Lied von der Erde* knows the moment of reflection on itself, as in "Der Trunkene im Frühling."[8] The first movement is a in bar form; only toward the end,[9] shortly before the refrain, does the *Abgesang* return to the *Stollen*. The long concluding section, obscurely combined from two poems, interprets the stanza form as an alternation of broadly conceived, mutually corresponding fields. As if their proportions alone were not sufficient to organize prose-like formations musically, *ausdrucklos* (expressionless) parts in the manner of recitative are opposed to melodically firmer, highly expressive sections. What Wagner took out of circulation in the opera, forms—rediscovered—musical prose. Schoenberg employed the same procedure at about the same time in the Finale of the Second Quartet and after that continually wrote recitatives; in the larger stage works of the New Music, *Von heute auf morgen*, *Moses und Aron*, *Wozzeck*, and *Lulu*, they have also made an appearance. Their resurrection in the late Mahler can be explained by the discursive bent that occasionally tires of absolute-musical mediation: by the documentary impulse. *Das Lied von der Erde* rebels against pure forms. It is an intermediate type. Alexander Zemlinsky, in one of his own works, later gave it the name "Lyric Symphony"; its influence continued up to Berg's

Lyric Suite. Even the *Kindertotenlieder* were arranged architectonically, the last being a rudimentary finale. The conception of the song-symphony is highly adequate to Mahler's idea: a whole which, without reference to superordinate a priori patterns, grows together from individual events arranged in a significant order. As a latent center of energy, the *Kindertotenlieder*, from the Fourth Symphony on, transmit their radiations across the whole of Mahler's work. A quotation from them is concealed even in the Eighth Symphony, to whose landscape, despite the voices of the boys who have died young, they are remotest.[10] The Symphony's specific relation to *Das Lied von der Erde*, however, is likely to be found in the experience that in youth infinitely much is apprehended as a promise of life, as anticipated happiness, of which the ageing person recognizes, through memory, that in reality the moments of such promise were life itself. The missed and lost possibility is rescued by the very late Mahler, by contemplating it through the inverted opera glass of childhood, in which it might still have been possible. Those moments are designated by the choice of the poems of the third, fourth, and fifth songs. The color of "Der Einsame im Herbst," the apotheosis of the orchestra of the *Kindertotenlieder*, is that of "old gold". As in the autumn poems of George's *Jahr der Seele*, decaying organic matter glistens metallically. The song on the pavilion, which ends like a transparent mirage, calls to mind the Chinese tale of the painter who vanishes into his picture, a trifling and inextinguishable pledge.[11] Diminution, disappearance is the guise of death, in which music still preserves the vanishing. "Friends, in fine attire, are drinking, talking," which they never really do, as in the miniature of memory, which promises it to those unborn. In such rejuvenation the dead are our children. The literary point of the poem of the pavilion, the mirror image, was beyond the power of music at the time *Das Lied von der Erde* was written. Mahler reacts to it with his inherited means, the minor mode, a melancholy episode. But how much it was the same point as that of his own conception is evident in the monstrous piece "Der Trunkene im Frühling." His situation is already the Expressionist one behind the mask of the objective ballad tone. The inner space is isolated, without a bridge to life, to which Mahler's music nevertheless clings with every fiber. With paradoxical realism the work thinks the situation through to its end, unveiled: the affinity to Proust lies in the interior monologue. The melancholy of the pool as a mirror is that to weltschmerz, which finally severs the threads, the real life that beckons appears as the dream that the first line of the poem invokes, whereas objectless inwardness turns itself into reality. When in a passage moving beyond all words the drunken man hears the voice of the bird, nature as an exhortation to the earth, he feels "as if dreaming." In vain he would go back once more. His solitude oscillates violently in his intoxication between despair and the joy of absolute freedom, already within the zone of death. The spirit of this music converges with Nietzsche, whom Mahler admired in his youth.[12] But where the Dionysus of the objectlessly inward set up his tablets with imperious impotence, Mahler's music escapes hubris by reflecting on its own cry, including within the composition laughter at its untruth. The intoxication of self-destruction, the heart that cannot contain itself pours itself out to that from which it is separated. Its downfall aims at reconciliation. The Adagio Finale of the Ninth Symphony, in the last phrase of the first D-flat major paragraph, for example, has the same tone of the rapture of self-surrender.[13] However, the drunken man's ecstasy, imitated by the music, lets in death through the gaps between notes and chords. Music catches up in Mahler with the shudder of Poe and Baudelaire, the *goût du néant*, as if it had become the alienation of one's own body: *Das Lied von der Erde* is brought in from the region of that madness before which the interjections in the autograph of the Tenth Symphony tremble. In "Der Abschied" the illusion of happiness, up to then the vital element of all music, disperses. Because happiness is sacred, the music no longer pretends that it already exists. Nothing of it remains except the gratified relaxation of one who has nothing more to lose; to the affirmative people that amounts to a lack of ethos. Nor is the tone of the movement that of despair. Prose shaken by sobs in the midst of tonality, it weeps without reason like one overcome by remembrance; no weeping had more reason. The musical fields within it are pages of a diary, each tense within itself, some rising upward, but none supported by the others, turning like pages in mere time, whose mourning music imitates. Hardly anywhere else does Mahler's music dissociate itself so unreservedly; the natural sounds mingle in anarchic groups, potentiate Mahler's old expression mark, *Ohne Rücksicht auf das Tempo* (without regard to the tempo).[14] Frequently the music grows tired of itself and gapes open:[15] then the inner flow carries the movement over the exhaustion of the outward one; emptiness itself becomes music. Only very late did the New Music again compose silence in this way. There is also vertical dissociation: the chords decay into parts. The contrasting device of the recitative infects the always sparely woven whole; the instruments disperse, as if each wanted to speak by itself, unheard. But the stuttering *ewig* (forever) at the end, repeated, as if the composition had laid down the wand of office, is not pantheism, which opens the view on blissful distances. No one-and-all is conjured up as consolation. The title *Das Lied von der Erde* might be suspected of complicity with those from the New German sphere such as "Nature Symphony" or even "Das hohe Lied vom Leben und Sterben," if the work's content did not as much justify the extraordinary claim of its title as it effaces its pompous aspect by its mourning truth. It is enabled to do so not least by the atmosphere which the music itself confers on the word *Erde*. It is said in the first Song that the earth has long—not forever—stood firm, and the leave-taker in "Der Abschied" even calls it the dear earth, as something vanishing that is embraced. To the work the earth is not the universe, but what fifty years later could fall within the experience of one flying at a great altitude, a star. For the gaze of music that leaves it behind, it is rounded to a sphere that can be overviewed, as in the meantime it has already been photographed from space, not the center of Creation but something minute and ephemeral. To such experience is allied the melancholy hope for other stars, inhabited by happier beings than humans. But the earth that has grown remote to itself is without the hope the stars once promised. It is sinking into empty galaxies. On it lies beauty as the reflection of past hope, which fills the dying eye until it is frozen below the flakes of unbound space. The moment of delight before such beauty dares to withstand its abandonment to disenchanted nature. That metaphysics is no longer possible becomes the ultimate metaphysics.

The splendor of immediate life reflected in the medium of memory
is as manifest in the first movement of the Ninth symphony, a piece
of purely instrumental music, as in *Das Lied von der Erde,* where it
receives added commentary from the text. But absolute music, playing from present to present, can never be purely remembrance.
This provides the inspiration for the first movement of the Ninth,
Mahler's masterpiece. Winfried Zillig has pointed out that its full
450 measures really consist from beginning to end of a single melody. It is "through-melodized" (*durchmelodisiert*) throughout. All
boundaries between phrases are blurred: musical language passes
entirely into the discursive voice. But where the melodic lines over-
lie each other and cross, they murmur as in dreams. Thus the collective seeks admission to the symphony of the departed one (*des Ab-
geschiedenen*) and founds the narrative voice. Telling of the past, the
wholly epic voice is heard. It begins as if something were to be narrated, yet concealed, as at the beginning of the Finale of the Sixth
Symphony the curtain rises over something ineffable and invisible.
The whole movement is inclined to one-measure beginnings; in
them the delivery is slightly impeded, as by the constricted breathing of the narrator. The almost labored one-measure steps of the
narrative carry the burden of the symphony's momentum at the
start of the Funeral March[16] like a coffin in a slow cortège. The bells
here are not Christian ones: with such malign pomp a mandarin is
buried. Yet as the movement, before this, involves itself with time, it
becomes entangled in immediacy, in a second life, blooming as if it
were the first: "Oft bin ich mir kaum bewußt, daß die wilde Freude
zücket." ("Often I almost swoon as wild joy leaps within me.") The
music develops by losing the detachment with which it began. It
goes back into the world, passing with the third theme of the exposition into manifest passion. Memory forgets to reflect on itself until
deceiving immediacy receives at its height a terrible blow, the me-
mento of fragility. Its hands retain nothing but ruins and a dubious
flattering solace: music draws fatally back into itself. Hence the recapitulation of a movement that otherwise, as Erwin Ratz has
shown, stands askew to the sonata. The sensuous consolation of the
very late Mahler has a dubious quality because it is bestowed solely

on such moments of retrospection and not on the present: only as memory does life have sweetness, and precisely that is pain. The rhythm of the catastrophe, however, is the same as the almost inaudibly quiet one of the first notes, as if it were only making manifestly real what secretly precedes the whole, the judgment on immediate life. Where it is entirely present, entirely itself, it reveals itself as given up to death.

The technical procedures exactly fit the content. The conflict with the schemata is decided against the latter. No more than the sonata idea is that of variations adequate to the piece.[17] Nevertheless, the alternating minor theme, whose contrast to the major region is maintained throughout the whole movement, appears—through the metrical similarity of its short phrases to those of the main theme and despite its different interval content—to be a variation on this theme. That too is antischematic; instead of making the contrasting theme stand out structurally from what precedes it, Mahler uses similar structures and displaces the contrast to the mode alone. In both themes, in keeping with the radicalized principle of the variant, the intervals are not determined, but only the flow and certain fixed notes. Similarity and contrast are both removed from the small cells and assigned to the thematic whole. The form might well be summed up by the concept of symphonic dialogue. In such terms Wagner spoke of the orchestral works that were all that he intended to write after completing *Parsifal*; it is not unlikely that the widely read Mahler knew of this and recognized in Wagner's project affinities with his own music, once this had broken away from the canon of forms: Alfred Casella was right, in disagreement with Guido Adler, that a new phase in Mahler dates from *Das Lied von der Erde*. If the much-quoted thematic dualism could only with difficulty be attributed to pre-Mahlerian symphonic writing by analogy to the drama, it is fully realized only by the epic composer; the great Andante of the Ninth Symphony is constructed on the proportions of the first and second themes. The short phrases are themselves potentially parts of a dialogue. They admit answers and need them for their completion. The tendency toward dialogue is imparted to the whole both by the manner of composing permanently overlapping parts, and by the major-minor antithesis: everywhere one and two main voices interchange iridescently. The omnipresent antithetical quality makes a development, as a sphere reserved for colliding opposites, superfluous; thus the liquidation of sonata form by the New Music is initiated in Mahler's Ninth. After the Eighth Mahler wrote as few real sonata movements as the mature Alban Berg. The second theme gives the impression of a minor version of the first, and hardly that of a second subject, although the third unmistakably condenses the character of a closing section. The repetition of the exposition is elaborated so far in terms of permanent variants that it is perceived spontaneously as a first part of a development; only through retrospective listening does it become clear what the development really ought to be. The consistency of Mahler's sense of form in the new phase is demonstrated by details such as the fact that in the disintegrating recapitulation of the movement, after the catastrophe, there is formed a prolonged cadenza-like solo duet between a flute and a horn treated with unprecedented audacity, accompanied on the low strings: the dualism originally inferred from major and minor is finally brought back to its ideal type, an undisguised two-part composition. In these measures Mahler reduces the disintegration fields to the fully elaborated cadenza; as such the fields grow eloquent and revert at last to their historical origin. In so doing he masterfully ignores the rule of composition according to which the horn should continually be given pauses for breathing. The horn melody is spun out in a single thread. It is suspended midway between recitative and theme as in the last piece of *Das Lied von der Erde*. The elaboration of melody finally becomes a formal category sui generis, the synthesis of thematic work and eloquence. In the movement's inclination toward dialogue its content appears. The voices interrupt each other, as if they wanted to drown each other out; hence the insatiable expression and the speech-like quality of the piece, of the absolute novel-symphony. The themes are neither active, precisely set in place, nor do they occur passively, but issue forth as if the music only while speaking received the impulse to speak on.

The thematic rhythms on which the work's unity is founded became the models for those in Berg's *Wozzeck*, his Chamber Concerto, and finally the *monoritmica* in *Lulu:* the serial incorporation of rhythm in structure has its origin in that movement. The construction of the main theme is also in the future perfect. It is led from unobtrusive beginnings uncharacteristic of a recitative to a mighty climax, a theme resulting from itself, as is only quite evident on retrospective listening. Schoenberg proceeded no differently in the first movement of his Violin Concerto, and such innovations in the language of forms are proving more relevant today than the stock of pitch material. The theme groups are, it is true, composed in a sharply antithetical manner, but are related in terms of motivic content in a violation of the rules betraying genius: one of the main rhythms[18] occurs in both the major and minor sectors, and altogether the two appear like variants of a tacit fundamental idea—an effect increased by the division into short sections common to both. Contours are both given emphasis marks and slurred, as if the musical *prosateur* suspected arbitrariness in the unambiguity of the musical fields that he nevertheless needs. The movement operates throughout with lengthened measures, not merely as preludes but as idling postludes, which soften the boundaries without acting as transitions.[19] In the alternating main complexes are embedded motivic components that later take on an independent existence. The subsidiary idea of the cellos,[20] to begin with a variant of a part of the main theme, then serves, in heavily modified form, as a kind of transition between the fields.[21] Independent of any fixed place in the schema, a motive very easily remembered through its chromaticism as well as its alternation of triplets with a dotted rhythm becomes ubiquitous. An invention of the spirit of the brass, it migrates through the whole orchestra. It is in keeping with its wandering character that despite its striking precision it is never firmly, definitively formulated. It is not placed simply as such in the foreground, but is first the closing element of a four-measure horn counterpoint to the minor theme before it penetrates the trumpet and prepares the fortissimo climax of the main theme.[22] The whole exposition closes with a theme of utmost intensity. Its form is something like that of a closing section.[23] Although it too is rhythmically derivative,[24] it makes the same impression as the new novel-figure in the second movement of the Fifth: as the critical figure of the movement. With a usually luxuriating accompaniment, in a sense it brings about the catastrophe as its own negation. On the first occasion it does not break the strength of the movement,[25] which then again rears leidenschaftlich (passionately) upwards; the chord D–F–A–C♯ that appears here, the absolute basis of the minor complex, became the leading sonority of the first Orchestral Piece of Schoenberg's op. 16. Finally, more disruptively than even the hammer earlier, the main rhythm, at the second attempt, intrudes into the heavy brass with the bass drum and the tam-tam.[26] Even the harmony over the low E-flat, before the first peak of the section in minor,[27] seems to penetrate too deeply into the musical body. The dazzling theme of the closing section becomes, at the end of the movement, appeased, a lustrous solace. Someone who is known to be dying is assured, as if he were a child, that all will be well. The whole movement is the epic enactment of "Mir war in dieser Welt das Glück nicht hold" from *Das Lied von der Erde*, which is heard two measures before the first minor entry. The field that directly follows the exposition and is introduced by the catastrophe rhythm on the horns,[28] is also prefigured in *Das Lied von der Erde*, in the atomized passages of "Der Abschied"; colors daubed on with the palette knife, superimposed layers of piano and fortissimo heighten the section without the use of heavy tutti to a threatening extreme.[29] The ragged field leads into a false recapitulation that runs its course while using the subsidiary idea, and only at the entry marked *Mit Wut* (Furiously)[30] gives way to a development leading to the first catastrophe. After the catastrophe the section in minor is repeated in a B-flat minor variant,[31] which resembles a development toward its end; it is followed by a de-realized dissolution field, then another recapitulation in the main key, heightened in the last section of the development to the point of catastrophe. The funeral march episode leads to the final recapitulation, which departs very widely from the original form.

The formulas of the late style are valid not as forms inherited no matter how, but as figures stamped out of the composer's will. This makes possible the instrumentation, which is now entirely a constituent means of representation in the music. The cellos quietly initiate the dotted rhythm of the opening. They are answered in syncopated form by the same A on the low horn; aside from the rhythm only the timbre changes a rudimentary melody of tone color. In the third measure the harp plays the *Urmotiv* of *Das Lied von der Erde* in inverted form; its forte is not quite real against the indistinct piano. The dynamics are divergent yet constrained, with a resonance whose hollowness can be created only by performance. While the rhythmic pattern of the cellos and the fourth horn continues, in the fourth measure a muted horn—again in a color at once different and similar—intones a new rhythm derived from the syncopated one; the motive that fills it is the same, essential one common to the two later main theme groups. In the fifth measure, again unconnectedly, an unmistakably accompanimental sextuplet figure on the violas is added; it persists as far as the second main theme group. After the first entry of this figure the second horn varies, now openly, the cadence of its essential motive.[32] Then it sinks into the background duet of the accompaniment; the entry of the main theme itself, in the second violins, is linked to it through contrary motion. Each instrument shuns the prescribed parallel to the other. Paradoxically, this introduction is rounded to a unity by virtue of a sustained divergence in all directions. In Mahler, the antithesis of disintegration and integration at the same time includes their identity: the centrifugal elements of the music, no longer to be restrained by any clamp, resemble each other and are articulated into a second whole. The disintegrating element of the introduction continues to exert its influence at the beginning of the first theme, over the tonic and in a distinct D major. While the theme seems comfortingly near, as if the music had reached native soil, the underlying tone remains somber—through the simplest instrumental means, such as that the accompanying pizzicati are reserved solely to the double basses in the low register, without being lightened by those of the cellos. The movement cannot shake off this disquieting and menacing atmosphere, like Kafka a tormenting dream yet excessively real; the catastrophe verifies this tone, as if secretly it had always been known and nothing else were expected. The dissociative tendency continues to produce the instrumental primary color of the entire movement, a kind of strangled mute forte: with the music, the sound itself is broken. The clattering D minor chord in the heavy brass, bassoons, double bassoon and timpani accompanying the minor theme[33] is this sound's paradigm. Only the passages that squander themselves toward the catastrophes are unfaithful to it. Toward the end of the movement, from about the solo passage after the last hint of the minor theme,[34] the color mimics the formal meaning of what has happened: as if the movement were already over, it loses all volume, the music holding itself like an astral body, *Schwebend* (floating) finally in accordance with Mahler's prescription. The continuation of the movement in disconnected breaths is everywhere traceable, even where the melodic lines have already been long spun out; similarly, one feels in the first movement of the Sixth Symphony, again and again throughout whole complexes, the soundless march rhythm, as if the composer had periodically turned away from his own piece. For just this reason, in the performance of the first movement of the Ninth, the danger of a trotting gait must be avoided by constant readiness to accentuate the up-beats instead of the strong beats of measures, as is suggested at the beginning of the development by Mahler's own dynamic markings, as soon as the seconds of the main motive reach the trombones.[35]

The second movement is a development-scherzo like those of the Fifth and Seventh, with three main groups strongly distinguished this time by tempo as well, the *Ländler* in C major, a much quicker waltz in E major,[36] and a quasi upper-Austrian, slow-motion *Ländler* theme in F;[37] the motive components of the groups are then tirelessly combined. The spirit of the Scherzo, however, has no model, even in Mahler. The *Ländler* main section is probably the first exemplary case of musical montage, anticipating Stravinsky both by its quotation-like themes and by its decomposition and lop-sided reunification. The tone of such montage, however, is not one of parody but rather one of a dance of death, more serenely struck in the Fourth. The fragments of the themes reassemble into a damaged afterlife, begin to swarm in a way distantly similar to that of the Scherzo of Beethoven's op. 135. To this is added in the faster parts of the waltz the despairing expression of that abasement to which the trio of the Seventh was subjected. Through its irreconcilable and obtrusive negativity, the movement, despite the traditional dance forms, is miraculously ahead of its time. And all the while it splits hairs even in hell, like Karl Kraus. The main theme group is merely a collage picture made from deformed clichés: it pillories reified, petrified forms. The musical intention emerges in the waltz section. This proceeds much more directly, also more seamlessly in terms of motives, yet shocks through the reeling, overenergetic harmony of "Der Trunkene im Frühling" and by its wild vulgarisms.[38] Finally, components of the first theme are counterpointed to the third. The Scherzo remains dynamic, does not take delight in the mere montage of senselessly ossified, immobile elements, but carries these with it in symphonic time, thereby making them again commensurable with the subject. The frisson in such a conception of music was repressed by the Surrealist Stravinsky: only symphonic time makes legible the horror of what time has lost, like Peter Schlemihl his shadow.

Confronted with this, the *Rondo* Burlesque, the name of which announces that it intends to laugh at the world's course, finds itself bereft of laughter. It is Mahler's one virtuoso piece, musically no less than orchestrally, devoid of all vestiges of solid craftmanship even in the fugato passages. They are not conspicuous as such, unlike those in the Finale of the Fifth and the first movement of the Eighth, but are subtly concealed by the principle of the double fugue, making merely more dense the already thoroughly integrated movement. After the Hymn of the Eighth, the ceremonial pretensions of the obviously fugal manner were antipathetic to Mahler. The mature master of counterpoint stumbles on the fact that fugues can no longer be written. The movement, which, despite its length, rushes past, does not present the world's course as something alien and painful to the ego, but as if it were internalized in the subject, as if the subject were himself enslaved to it, and so was of as little concern to it as spring to the drunken man. No longer do the others hasten, under the gaze of a musical ego that believes itself better. Rather, the entangled subject can no longer remain outside: the world's course brings desolation into the subject's own heart. Only to music is it granted so to intermingle earthly life and the compulsion to die. Where the notation changes from alla breve to 2/4 time, while the tempo is strictly maintained, one of the main motives of the Rondo is revealed as a theme in its own right.[39] It saunters to the rhythm of the "Women" song in the *Merry Widow*, which at that time squeaked from the brass horns of phonographs. Thus does Proust deport himself in those photographs showing him as a bon vivant with top hat and jauntily flourished cane: the incognito of the genius who destroys himself by mingling in the shallow life of others. Only the Allegro misterioso from Berg's *Lyric Suite* is a comparable virtuoso piece on despair. Virtuosity and despair, however, attract each other. For the former is always poised on the brink of failure, of plunging as if from the pinnacle of the circus tent; at each moment the virtuoso can make a slip, be ejected from the closed formation that the movement presents to the outside. With the slightest mistake the whole founders, so closely are technical procedure and expression united. The question "What does the world cost?," with which Mahler is said to have explicated the Seventh Symphony, is also answered by the Burlesque of the Ninth: nothing. But it is the question of the gambler who in the long run must lose to the bank. To buy the world is bankruptcy. Virtuosity, absolute mastery as play, condemns the master at the same time to total impotence. In all virtuosity, including that of composition, the subject defines itself as a mere medium and so blindly subjects itself to what it aspires to subjugate. The episode of the breakthrough has become as fruitless in the Burlesque as the hope of the opening window at the death of Josef K. in *The Trial*, a mere fluttering of the good life that is possible but is not:

> With a flicker as of a light going up, the casements of a window there suddenly flew open; a human figure, faint and insubstantial at that distance and that height, leaned abruptly far forward and stretched both arms still farther.[40]

No more is "Der Trunkene im Frühling" awakened by the bird song, which has its echo in the sound and even the themes of the Burlesque episode;[41] so entirely is the subject alienated from itself that it finds no way back: truth appears to it as phantasmagoria. Through being a counterpoint from the last fugato,[42] the episode theme confesses itself a reflection of the immanence that nourishes all transcendental images and so poisons them. In Mahler's world of images hope has grown very poor, its extraneousness to the work a vanishing trace in the depths of its caves.

The Burlesque goes back to the Fifth even in its motives. It is not uncommon in Mahler for the same materials to give rise to quite different characters, as in the Scherzo of the Fifth, where the darkly solemn theme of the second trio is idyllically illuminated in the transition to A-flat major.[43] The Burlesque has a reckless gaiety, as if at any moment it might plunge into a bottomless void. On the second appearance of the alternative theme there is a striking and truly terrible horn passage,[44] warbling like the old-fashioned hit song "In der Nacht, wenn die Liebe erwacht," taking on a melancholy quality through the use of heavy instruments to play the commonplace, happy melody. Its disproportion to the motivic content causes it to gasp apoplectically. Besides, the virtuoso treatment of the brass in the Ninth Symphony strips that family of instruments entirely of its magic: hustling solemnity is already a groan of fear. Once more in the episode of the movement solace and despair intersect, not in a murkily blurred manner but distinctly, like the contrasting dots of orchestral color in the Ninth. It is only such passages that enact the kaleidoscopic fantasy that early German Romanticism hoped for from music. The bondage of the drunkard is one with the delusion connected with unbroken immanence. Even the giddy quality of the harmony becomes part of it as a factor of deception and an element of language. The Ninth Symphony accommodates this element not only in the Burlesque but equally in the waltz theme of the second movement; in Mahler, too, what was expressive character becomes material. Analogously to earlier Schoenberg, the bass line is strengthened and at the same time incorporates the chromatic. The life of tonality is at stake. Scale degrees, now autonomous, become dissociated from each other in their immediate sequence; only by force could they be analyzed by Riemann's method. In this too dissociation and construction mediate each other. The energetic advance of a movement that is held together in a tighter unity than any other by Mahler is made possible equally by the strong bass line and by its faltering, two contradictory aspects of the same situation, as if relentless unheeding progress were from the outset the path to perdition.

The Adagio Finale is reluctant to close, as was Berg's *Lyric Suite* after it, to the extent that it remained an artistic fragment. Yet this tendency is limited within the form by the relation to the first movement, which, despite its constant inclination toward allegro, is likewise slow. Over and above the tempo, the two movements are structurally matched in that both, in the course of the recapitulation, divest the themes of their fixed certainty, finally presenting only fragments of them. This reinforces the character of retrospection, of a no longer restrained, fitfully intruding memory. Such merely structural similarity between musical fields, in which no compact measure remains and air penetrates everywhere, creates an architectonic symmetry even without motivic connections. The sense of something awesome, which leaves the listener at the end still holding his breath, is rather a consciousness produced after the event than something located in a direct musical presence. As if across aeons, the phrase "Im Himmel sein" from the *Urlicht* of the Second Symphony returns at the beginning.[45] But as if in extreme old age, steeped in experience and already growing remote from it, the movement gazes backwards, a music of detached reminiscence. As if it were half forgotten, the melody of the "long, long way" from the *Kindertotenlieder* divides into two violin parts;[46] the episode theme of the Burlesque is, to begin with, concealed in a middle part in the Adagio.[47] The Mahlerian transcendence of yearning itself speaks, in unrepeatable tones, in the melody of the first violins stretched over two octaves, one measure earlier. The formal idea pays homage to Bruckner in the increasingly richly adorned return of the same main complex after contrasting sections. However, not only is this return purified of everything mechanical, of the merely external intensification that mars Bruckner's adagio type even in his late period; not only is Mahler's art of the variant doubly concerned, in a movement operating with a relatively limited stock of motives, to avoid any repetition, most of all, perhaps, in the continuation of the last return of the main theme[48]—but the Brucknerian structure, which sometimes determines the treatment of the counterpoint,[49] is modified by an extremely novel formal idea. After the first eight-measure phrase of the main theme there appears a two-measure interpolation by the solo bassoon in D-flat minor. It returns twice more notated in C-sharp minor, spreads itself as a theme complex in its own right, something evolving, as against the static first theme that was merely deflected by variants. By this means the extremely slow piece is assimilated to Mahler's dynamic sense of time. Up to its third, decisive appearance[50] the C-sharp minor complex confesses itself through sound and motive —the thirds played by clarinets and harp in unison, the solo woodwinds, the avoidance of string tutti—to be of one mind with the "Der Abschied" in *Das Lied von der Erde*. The re-entry of the string chorus with the second strophe of the main theme is marked by Mahler as *heftig ausbrechend* (breaking out violently):[51] irresistibly remembering. This retrospective turn is followed by the whole recapitulation. The revoked time no longer has a goal, leads nowhere, the cadence losing itself entirely. However, even this movement admits the pedestrianness of four-part trombone passages, an apotheosis of the male choir. The parting, however, is without the solemnity of the main theme, only scattered groups of notes remaining, among them the motive from the *Kindertotenlieder*.[52] The leave-taking music cannot break away. But not because it wants to appropriate, to assert itself. The subject cannot detach contemplative love from the irrecoverable. The long gaze is fastened on the condemned. Since his awkward youthful composition with piano accompaniment on the folk song "Zu Straßburg auf der Schanz," Mahler's music has sympathized with the social outcasts who vainly stretch out their hands to the collective. "Ich soll dich bitten um Pardon, und ich bekomm' doch meinen Lohn! Das weiss ich schon" (Though I should ask your pardon I shall get my deserts, I know full well). Mahler's music is subjective not as his expression, but in that he puts it in the mouth of a deserter. All are last words. The man to be executed deafeningly utters what he has to say, without anyone hearing. Only so that it is said. Music admits that the fate of the world no longer depends on the individual, but it also knows that this individual is capable of no content except his own, however fragmented and impotent. Hence his fractures are the script of truth. In them the social movement appears negatively, as in its victims. Even the marches in these symphonies are heard and reflected by those whom they drag away. Only those cast from the ranks, tramped underfoot, the lost outpost, the one buried "where the shining trumpets blow," the poor "drummer boy," those wholly unfree for Mahler embody freedom. Bereft of promises, his symphonies are ballads of the defeated, for "Nacht ist jetzt schon bald"—soon the night will fall.

NOTES

All of Mahler's orchestral works are quoted from the study scores. The First to Fourth, Eighth, and Ninth Symphonies and *Das Lied von der Erde* were published by Universal Edition, Vienna. The *Wunderhorn* songs, the *Kindertotenlieder,* and the so-called *Sieben Lieder aus letzter Zeit* are in the Philharmonia series of scores. The publisher of the Fifth Symphony is Peters, Leipzig; of the Sixth, C. F. Kahnt Nachfolger, Leipzig; of the Seventh, Bote und Bock, Berlin. For the same publisher Edwin Ratz brought out the revised edition in 1960. Three volumes of piano songs have been published by Schott Söhne, Mainz.*

1
---

1. 1/I, 5 after [1].

2. 1/I, 9 after [25].

3. 4/IV, 7 after [1].

4. Hegel, *Phänomenologie des Geistes,* ed. Lasson (Leipzig, 1921), 250.

5. 2/III, 10 after [50] ff.

---

*Adorno cited page numbers in the editions he used. To make it easier to follow his references in other editions, citations have been changed to measure numbers counted in relation to rehearsal numbers, in brackets ("one after . . ." begins the count with the measure of the rehearsal number). All references are to symphonies unless otherwise indicated: 1/I, 5 after [1] indicates First Symphony, first movement, 5 measures after rehearsal number 1. In the Sixth Symphony, the Scherzo is counted as movement II and the Andante movement III.—*Trans.*

6. 2/III, [37] ff.

7. 2/III, 12 after [37].

8. Natalie Bauer-Lechner, *Recollections of Gustav Mahler*, trans. Dika Newlin (London, 1980), 36–37.

9. 3/III, [16] ff. and [17] ff.

10. 3/III, 18 after [16] ff.

11. 3/III, [31] to [32].

12. 7/III, [116] to [118], [118] to [120], 2 after [154] to 1 after [156].

13. 4/II, [11] ff.

14. Cf. Paul Bekker, *Gustav Mahlers Sinfonien* (Berlin, 1921), 181.

15. 5/II, opening performance direction.

16. 1/I, 5 after [12] ff.

17. 1/I, 3 after [15] with up-beat.

18. 1/I, [26] ff.

19. Hegel, *Science of Logic*, trans. W. H. Johnson and L. G. Struthers (London, 1929), 87.

20. Hegel, *Wissenschaft der Logik* I (Sämtliche Werke 4, ed. Glockner; Stuttgart, 1928), 510 ff.

21. Richard Wagner, *Gesammelte Schriften und Dichtungen* 6 (Leipzig, 1888), Der Ring des Nibelungen, 128.

22. Bauer-Lechner, *Recollections*, 160.

23. Ibid.; 1/IV, 14 before [45].

24. Bauer-Lechner, *Recollections*, 130.

2

1. 5/I, 5 ff. after [5] with up-beat.

2. 7/II, 5–6 after [134] with up-beat, or 2 before [137].

3. 5/I, 10 and 9 before [15].

4. Guido Adler, *Gustav Mahler* (Vienna, 1916), 50.

5. Columbia Long Playing Record 33⅓ CX 1250.

6. *Des Knaben Wunderhorn* (Leipzig, 1906), 702.

7. 3/V, 4 after [3], alto solo.

8. Arnold Schoenberg, *Style and Idea* (New York, 1950), 34.

9. Cf. T. W. Adorno, *Noten zur Literatur* (Frankfurt am Main, 1958), 144 ff.

10. Cf. T. W. Adorno, *Dissonanzen* (2nd ed., Göttingen, 1958), 44.

11. Schoenberg, *Style and Idea*, 23.

12. Cf. Arnold Schoenberg, *Briefe*, ed. Erwin Stein (Mainz, 1958), 271 ff.

13. Cf. T. W. Adorno, *Klangfiguren* (Frankfurt am Main, 1959), 297.

14. Bauer-Lechner, *Recollections*, 167.

15. 3/III, 9 after [14] with up-beat.

16. 3/III, [28], *wie nachhorchend*.

3

1. 4/I, [7] with cello up-beat; cf. also 9 after [23], *ruhig und immer ruhiger werdend*.

2. 4/III, 6 after [2] with up-beat.

3. Erwin Ratz, "Zum Formproblem bei Gustav Mahler. Eine Analyse des ersten Satzes der Neunten Symphonie," *Die Musikforschung* 8 (1955): 176.

4. 2/I, 5 after [12] ff.

5. 5/I, [18] to the return of C♯ minor, 9 after [19].

6. T. W. Adorno, "Schönbergs Bläserquintett," *Pult und Taktstock* 5 (May–June, 1928): 46 ff.

7. 5/IV, 5 after [1] *wieder äußerst langsam* and 1 after [4].

8. 2/I, first at [6] ff.

9. 9/II, [19] ff.

10. 5/I, 6 before [11] ff.

11. 5/I, 7 after [3].

12. 6/IV, 2 after [111].

13. 6/IV, 7 after [147] ff. with up-beat.

14. Wagner, *Gesammelte Schriften* 7, Tristan und Isolde, 30.

15. Cf. Adler, *Mahler*, 46.

16. 1/III, [6] ff.

17. 1/III, 1 after [16], *viel schneller*.

18. 4/I, 1 after [10] ff.

19. 4/III, beginning 2 before [2].
20. 4/I, 5 after [17] with up-beat.
21. 4/I, 3 after [1].
22. 4/I, 4 after [7], cellos.
23. 4/I, [16] ff.
24. 4/I, [19] ff.
25. 4/I, [2] ff.
26. 4/I, [18].
27. cf. 4/I, m. 6.
28. *Des Knaben Wunderhorn* 1/I, mm. 50 ff.
29. 4/I, m. 10 with up-beat.
30. 4/IV, [10].
31. 4/I, 11 after [24].

4

1. 5/V, the 4 mm. before [1].
2. Bekker, *Mahlers Sinfonien*, 16.
3. Ibid., 17–18.
4. Cf. Bauer-Lechner, *Recollections*, 147.
5. Ernst Bloch, *Geist der Utopie* (Berlin, 1923), 83.
6. 9/I, 12 after [6] ff.
7. 4/I, the 3 mm. before [8].
8. Cf. Adler, *Mahler*, 43.
9. e.g. 5/II, around [11].
10. cf. 7/III, opening; 9/I, 12 after [13].
11. 5/II, [3] ff. (trumpet 1).
12. 5/II, 5 after [16] ff.
13. Mahler, *Des Knaben Wunderhorn*.
14. Ibid.
15. Bekker, *Mahlers Sinfonien*, 23–24.
16. Goethe, *Sämtliche Werke* (Jubiläumsausgabe, Stuttgart and Berlin), 36: 247.
17. 5/II, 4 before [9].

18. Cf. Max Horkheimer and T. W. Adorno, *Dialektik der Aufklärung* (Amsterdam, 1947), 97.

19. 3/I, the 6 mm. before [13].

20. 3/I, [54] to [55].

21. 3/I, [62] ff.

22. First appearing 3/I, 5 after [11] ff. (oboe); esp. cf. 5 after [18] ff.

23. 3/I, [43] ff.

24. cf. e.g. 3/I, [26] ff.

25. 3/I, [27].

26. 3/I, [28].

27. 3/I, 12 after [28].

28. 3/I, [53] to [55] and previously.

29. 3/I, [29] ff.

30. 3/I, [34] ff.

31. 3/I, 5 before [35] to [39].

32. 3/I, [39] to [43].

33. 3/I, [43] ff.

5

1. Cf. Bauer-Lechner, *Recollections*, 40.

2. 7/I, [42]; 4 after [46].

3. 3/I, 5 after [2]; 6/IV, 3 after [104].

4. 2/III, 5 before [30].

5. 4/I, m. 5.

6. 4/I, m. 9 (viola sixteenth notes).

7. 4/I, m. 13.

8. 4/I, 5 before [2].

9. 4/I, 3 before [2].

10. 4/I, 8 after [18].

11. 4/I, 4 and 6 after [23]; cf. 1 and 2 after [23].

12. 9/I, 6 before [3].

13. Cf. Ratz, "Zum Formproblem," 172 ff.

14. 9/I, 9–10 after [3] (first appearance).

15. 9/I, 52–53 after [16] (horn 1).

16. 6/IV, from about 5 after [145] ff., distinctly from 2 before [147].

17. 6/IV, [153] ff.

18. 6/IV, [106] ff.

19. 6/IV, [109] ff.; cf. up-beat to [134] ff.

20. 6/IV, [110] ff.

21. 6/IV, 3 after [113].

22. 6/IV, [117].

23. 6/IV, [120] ff.

24. Cf. J. P. Jacobsen, *Gesammelte Werke*, 1: Novellen, Briefe, Gedichte, Brief an Ed. Brandes, 6. February 1878 (Jena and Leipzig, 1905), 247.

25. 6/IV, [123] ff.

26. 6/IV, [134] ff.

27. 6/IV, [129] ff.

28. 6/IV, 5 after [133] ff.

29. 6/IV, 3 after [116] ff.

30. 6/IV, 3 before [134].

31. 6/IV, 1 after [116].

32. 6/IV, [134] ff.

33. 6/IV, [140] ff.

34. 6/IV, [164] ff.

35. 7/I, 3 after [2] ff.

36. Bruckner, 9/III, [A].

37. 7/I, 3 after [3].

38. 7/I, e.g. [7] to [9]; or [20].

39. 7/I, the G major 5 after [33].

40. 1/II, [18] to [19]; [22] ff.

41. 1/II, up to [20].

42. 1/II, 2 before [9]; and 7–8 after [9].

43. Cf. Bauer-Lechner, *Recollections*, 172–73.

44. 5/III, 4 before [32] ff., *noch rascher*.

45. 5/III, up-beat to [1].

46. 5/III, [5] ff.

47. 5/III, [11] ff.

48. 5/III, 22 after [11].

49. 6/II, [51] ff.

50. 7/III, 3 after [163] with up-beat.

51. 7/III, [165] ff. with up-beat.

6

1. 4/II, [8] ff.

2. 3/II, 6 before [2].

3. 3/I, 5 after [4].

4. e.g. 3/I, 7 after [5]; and esp. [7] ff.

5. *Wunderhorn* 1/I, m. 21 (4/4 measure).

6. *Wunderhorn* 1/I, m. 107.

7. 7/I, 4–5 after [16].

8. 7/III, 4 after [217] to [218].

9. 5/III, [10] ff.

10. 5/III, 5 before [28] ff.

11. Bauer-Lechner, *Recollections*, 162.

12. Ibid., 147.

13. Ibid., 155–56.

14. 1/III, [3] ff.

15. Cf. Adorno, "Die Funktion des Kontrapunkts in der Neuen Musik," in *Klangfiguren*, 210 ff.

16. cf. 9/II, 10 after [17] with up-beat (violin 2); [18] ff. (cellos).

17. e.g. 1/II, [23] ff.

18. Bekker, *Mahlers Sinfonien*, 28.

19. 3/I, [15] to [16].

20. 3/I, [16] ff.

21. 1/IV, 4 and 3 before [13]; cf. next two mm.

22. 8/I, [23] to [30].

23. 8/I, esp. [26] to [27].

24. 4/III, the 7 mm. before [2].

25. 5/III, 2 after [10] ff.

26. Cf. Egon Wellesz, "Mahlers Instrumentation," *Anbruch* 12 (1930): 109.

7

1. 6/I, [25].

2. *Das Lied von der Erde*/VI, [40].

3. Erwin Ratz, "Zum Formproblem bei Gustav Mahler. Eine Analyse des Finales der VI. Symphonie," *Die Musikforschung* 9 (1956): 166.

4. 6/I, [37] ff.

5. Cf. Ratz, "Zum Formproblem . . . VI. Symphonie," 169–70.

6. *Gustav Mahler, Im eigenen Wort—Im Wort der Freunde*, ed. Willi Reich (Zurich, 1958), 73, quoted from *Die Fackel*, no. 324/25 (Vienna, 2 June 1911).

7. Cf. Bauer-Lechner, *Recollections*, 176–77.

8. Richard Wager, *Parsifal* (Kleine Orchesterpartitur, Mainz, Vienna, Leipzig, n.d.), 27–28.

9. Cf. Horkheimer and Adorno, *Dialektik der Aufklärung*, 214–15.

10. 5/IV, 5 after [1].

11. Hegel, *Rechtsphilosophie*, ed. Glockner, 7: 35.

12. Hans F. Redlich, "Mahlers Wirkung in Zeit und Raum," *Anbruch* 12 (1930): 95.

13. Cf. Schoenberg, *Briefe*, 274.

14. 8/I, 2 before [2].

15. 8/II, [56] ff.

16. 8/II, 5 after [63] to 4 after [76].

17. Cf. T. W. Adorno, "Zur Schlußszene des Faust," *Akzente* 6 (1959): 570.

8

1. *Das Lied von der Erde*/IV, up-beat to 5 after [21].

2. Cf. Ernst Křenek and T. W. Adorno, "Kontroverse über Fortschritt und Reaktion," *Anbruch* 12 (1930): 191 ff.

3. *Das Lied von der Erde*/VI, 6 after [4] with up-beat.

4. *Das Lied von der Erde*/VI, 3 after [51] to [52].

5. 9/I, 5 after [1].

6. *Das Lied von der Erde*/I, 5–6 after [37].

7. 4/II, mm. 22 ff.

8. *Das Lied von der Erde*/V, 1 before [9] ff.

9. *Das Lied von der Erde*/I, [39].

10. 8/II, 2 before [120].

11. Cf. Ernst Bloch, *Spuren* (Frankfurt am Main, 1959), 191 ff.

12. Cf. Adler, *Mahler*, 43.

13. 9/IV, mm. 21 ff. (*fliessend*).

14. *Das Lied von der Erde*/VI, 3 before [21] ff.; [36] ff.

15. *Das Lied von der Erde*/VI, [37] ff.

16. 9/I, 12 after [15] ff.

17. Cf. Ratz, "Zum Formproblem . . . Neunten Symphonie," e.g. 177.

18. 9/I, m. 4; 8 before [4]; 15 after [5].

19. 9/I, first time 8–9 after [2].

20. 9/I, first time 3 before [4].

21. 9/I, 6 after [7] ff.; 13 after [8].

22. 9/I, 8 after [3] (horn 1 and 3); 10 after [3] (trumpet 1).

23. 9/I, 4 before [6] ff.

24. 9/I, 4–5 after [3].

25. 9/I, 6 before [11] ff.

26. 9/I, 8 before [15] ff.

27. 9/I, 3 after [3].

28. 9/I, 13 after [6] (the double bar).

29. 9/I, cf. esp. 13–14 after [6]; 5–7 mm. later; [7] ff. (horns and trombones).

30. 9/I, [9].

31. 9/I, 10 after [11].

32. 9/I, mm. 5–6.

33. 9/I, 7 before [3].

34. 9/I, 21 after [16] ff.

35. 9/I, 3–4 after [7].

36. 9/II, 33 after [18] (tempo II).

37. 9/II, 32 after [21] (tempo III).

38. 9/II, e.g. 12 before [20] ff.

39. 9/III, 12 before [31] ff.

40. Franz Kafka, *The Trial* (London, 1968), 254.

41. 9/III, 19 after [36] ff., clearest 4 before [37] ff.

42. 9/III, from the A-flat section 9 before [36] (violin 1).

43. 5/III, 30 after [11] (clarinet).

44. 9/III, the 9 mm. before [35].

45. 9/IV, mm. 7–8.

46. 9/IV, m. 15.

47. 9/IV, m. 24.

48. 9/IV, esp. mm. 140 ff.

49. 9/IV, mm. 64–65.

50. 9/IV, m. 98 (*stets sehr gehalten*).

51. 9/IV, mm. 117 ff.

52. 9/IV, mm. 166 ff.